Latin American Travel

THREE YEARS IN CHILE

by Mrs. George B. Merwin

Edited and with an Introduction

by C. HARVEY GARDINER

Southern Illinois University Press

CARBONDALE AND EDWARDSVILLE

Feffer and Simons, Inc.

LONDON AND AMSTERDAM

Contents

Introduction

The political tranquillity and economic prosperity which set Chile apart from the rest of Spanish America in mid-nineteenth-century years, and drew increasing foreign attention to that land, stemmed in large measure from men and policies of previous decades.

Onetime merchant Diego Portales, the individual who gave direction to many areas of Chilean life, had introduced economic and political programs which contributed unity and strength at home and dignity and esteem abroad. A conservative oligarchy seized and retained the political reins but their policies served well the desires of a progressive commercial community. An intimate friend and supporter of Portales, General Joaquín Prieto, occupied the presidency from 1831 to 1841. During his second five-year term the successful struggle against the Peruvian-Bolivian Confederation of Santa Cruz, after contributing to Chilean nationalism, ushered in a sound and stable peace.

General Manuel Bulnes, hero of that war of the late 1830's, opened new vistas for Chileans even though his conservative outlook persisted throughout the ten years (1841–1851) he served as president. Intellectual ferment promoted the founding of a normal school (1842) and a national university (1843), the former under the direction of Argentine-emigré Domingo Faustino Sarmiento and the latter under the leadership of Venezuela-born Andrés Bello. While the number of primary schools multiplied and various literary periodicals were mushrooming, other signs of Chilean progress evidenced themselves: a better credit rating abroad and a law of uniform weights and measures at home, among others. The government pushed its claims to the Strait of Magellan and also initiated foreign colonization by industrious Europeans. A few Chileans departed for California's gold fields; many more stayed at home to produce wheat for that profitable market.

In 1851 Manuel Montt, the cabinet officer who in the previous decade had wrought miracles in behalf of education, assumed the presidency. Conspicuous for his organizing ability, his administrative capacity and his efficiency, Montt ushered in another autocratic decade in which Chilean progress derived largely from continuity of political and economic outlook. During peaceful mid-century years noteworthy foreign influences came to Chile, many of them tinged with Anglo-Saxon origins.

Britons dominated the fields of finance, commerce, and transportation. Some of the American contributions vied unsuccessfully for the recognition they deserved: the multiple enterprises of Massachusetts-born William Wheelwright, whose transportation, gas, and water developments were invariably backed by British rather than American capital; and likewise the American Stagecoach Company, a transportation monopoly between Valparaiso and Santiago which was enjoyed by one B. F. Morse. Other mobile mid-century Americans, headed for California's gold fields via Cape Horn, but briefly glimpsed Chile, usually in the vicinity of Talcahuano.

Meanwhile, augmenting the South American nation's orientation toward Europe—and supplementing Britain's dominant position in reference to capital investment—were the Spanish dramas that succeeded one another in the theaters, the French novels and paintings that won widening favor among the intellectuals, and the Italian opera companies that set the vogue in music.

Travelers of many nationalities recorded their Chilean experiences in that period. George Byam's *Wanderings in Some of the Western Republics of America* set four years of Chilean experiences before his fellow-Englishmen. A horseman and ex-soldier, Byam gave considerable attention to the world of the out-of-doors man, as well as to

aspects of Chilean social life. Fred Walpole, a lieutenant
in Queen Victoria's navy, exhibited the condescending
hauteur of the self-proclaimed English gentleman. *Four
Years in the Pacific*, his "sketches of loitering days in glowing
climes, in sunshine, and in youth [his early twenties]"
teemed with cultural arrogance masked as sophistication.

To brief glimpses of Chile in 1846 and 1848, Lieutenant Isaac G. Strain of the U.S. Navy added the experiences of one month in 1849 before penning *Sketches of a
Journey in Chili, and the Argentine Provinces, in 1849*, a work
which, like most other travel accounts, wed historical
narrative and personal experience. Most visitors com-
mented upon the physical aspect of Valparaiso and Strain
reacted as had many others when he wrote, "The com-
bination of the two Spanish words *Val-paraiso*, it is well
known, means the Vale of Paradise; but why it should
have been applied to this particular locality, has sadly
puzzled the brains of many who insist upon appropriate-
ness in appellations." (More bitter was Walpole's comment: "I cling to the 'Va al Paraiso,' referring of course to
Quillota, a lovely valley some forty miles to the north-
ward, as nobody, save in a joke, could have called this the
Valley of Paradise.") The Italian operatic troupe which
Strain enjoyed would be there for Mrs. Merwin to hear
almost a decade later.

An Englishman on a world tour, S. S. Hill gave the
port-to-capital axis little more than two weeks of his time.
Five chapters of undistinguished reporting in his *Travels
in Peru and Mexico* record his Chilean experience.

For most travelers of this period the Chilean itin-
erary knew two ingredients: brief glimpses at certain port
cities—including Caldera and Coquimbo to the north of
Valparaiso and Talcahuano and Concepción to the south;
and that junketing ashore that invariably moved the
foreigner between the principal port and the national
capital.

To an overwhelmingly masculine company, of whom
the foregoing are but representative, an American woman

added a superior record of travel writing in the volume *Three Years in Chile*.

Three Years in Chili, as the book was styled for its initial publication in 1863, recounted the experiences of Mrs. George B. Merwin, wife of the U.S. Consul in Valparaiso. The strictly chronological coverage of her journey to Chile, including a vivid description of a tedious crossing of the Isthmus of Panama, gives way, soon after arrival in Chile, to a basically topical consideration of her stay in that country. "These sketches of my life in Valparaiso," as the author termed her work, occasionally exhibit abrupt transitions and odd juxtapositions of themes.

Lacking the earmarks of literary grace, the book, in its unhurried yet concise factual homespun, carries a convincing ring of sincerity. Although composed years later in reflective moments—and its organization attests an expenditure of effort, *Three Years in Chile*—to give the name of the country its more modern spelling—is more narrative than interpretive. It also is almost devoid of hearsay and significant reference to historical literature.

One contemporary traveler's writing on Chile, Lieutenant James M. Gilliss' *United States Naval Astronomical Expedition to the Southern Hemisphere during the Years 1849–1852*—published in 1855, Mrs. Merwin frankly admired. From it she even quoted briefly, on religion, education, and mining. The only historian whose works she admittedly employed was the eminent eighteenth-century Jesuit, Juan Ignacio Molina, some of whose writing had been translated into English in the dawning years of the nineteenth century.

In addition to its pervasive air of honest reporting, *Three Years in Chile* is further recommended by the diversity and multiplicity of its themes. In writing of her Panamanian travel, "We were cautioned to look into our shoes before putting them on in the morning, lest there should be scorpions in them, and always remembered the caution—just after tying them," the author injected a quiet humor which frequently recurs in the book. Perhaps it was defense of her sex—and then, too, she might have seen too many women working too hard—that led her to exclaim, "The women of this coast [the west coast of South America] are much superior to the men in point of intellect, activity, and what we should call go-ahead-ativeness." Admiration for the climate joined love of beauty when, one January in Valparaiso, she enthused over "straw-colored tea roses covering a wall ten feet high, and blooming in clusters of four or five, each rose the size of a coffee-saucer." Tidbits such as these possibly prompted Tom B. Jones (*South America Rediscovered*) to remark concerning Mrs. Merwin, "it is proverbial that a woman is likely to notice things that a mere man would never see, and for social history the feminine point of view has its advantages."

Her pro-and-con coverage is kaleidoscopic on occasion, as when she said, "now we were charmed with the delicious climate, and now disgusted with the dirty lanes and unwholesome people; now we shuddered at the throes of an earthquake, and now we bargained for poultry at the gate; now we mused among the groves of the pantheons, and now we strolled through the city diverted with its abounding and novel life." "All Chileno crowds, religious and secular, are distinguished by two things: an overpowering stench of garlic, and the presence of innumerable fleas," Mrs. Merwin insisted as she moved from specific instance to generalization.

In Santiago—for her observations were not restricted to Valparaiso—the consul's lady one day lifted her gaze above the Plaza de la Independencia to the crimson rays of the setting sun on majestic snow-capped peaks. Reveling in the almost breathtaking beauty, she affirmed that that one scene "repaid us a thousandfold for all we had endured in Chile."

Closing a consideration of the police of Valparaiso, she ventured the comparison, "On the whole, I think life and property are safer in the midnight streets of Valparaiso than in many cities of the United States." "If one had the arrangement of a climate to suit oneself, one could hardly make one more perfect than that of Chile," Mrs. Merwin insisted, despite having weathered fifty-eight earthquakes there.

Long-term observation and objectivity characterize such utterances on religion as these: "No progress is made in the conversion of the natives to Protestantism; and I do not see how there is to be a change in this respect" and "As in other Catholic countries, the priests here have the strongest hold upon the devout and emotional natures of the women."

Reviewing the position of women in Chilean life, much of which evoked regret and lament, the American observer entertained a questionable conclusion when she wrote, "In nine cases out of ten, married without consulting her wishes, she is an indifferent wife of an unfaithful husband." Admiration and humility also punctuated Mrs. Merwin's reactions, as when she wrote, "We profess to be a cultivated people and stiffen our necks with Yankee independence, but in some things we might learn courtesy from the Chilenos." She proceeded to recite specific instances.

In her mid-thirties at the time of her arrival in Chile, Loretta L. (Wood) Merwin was the prim daughter of the Anglo-Saxon parents who accompanied her. At the age of twenty, Loretta Wood had married George B. Merwin, in the summer of 1838. Their two sons, Noble and George, went to Chile with them. Possessed of an education which included a rich vocabulary—and a willingness to show her love of poetry, Mrs. Merwin repeatedly revealed her Yankee background—in her boundless curiosity, in her persistent yet quiet humor, and in her high moral tone. Her tendency to look down her nose induced the utterance: "The walls and fixtures [of our house] are all as black as a chimney flue and utterly revolting to the spirit of Yankee housekeeping within me."

Like all the others who went with her, Mrs. Merwin traveled to Chile totally ignorant of the Spanish language. That problem, as her book indicates, she at least partially overcame. Her total lack of preparation for Latin American life was apparent initially in her unsympathetic, even hostile and intolerant attitude. All this rapidly diminished and few if any negative reactions stemmed from religious grounds, even though her Protestantism shone through on occasion. Perhaps her tolerant approach to Chilean religious life was related to that measure of tolerance which had permitted the establishment of places of Protestant worship in Valparaiso. Some of her capacity for caustic criticism yielded to climatic charms and some to her progressively better understanding of the antecedents—the cultural logic—of prevailing manners and customs.

All of the Merwins had gone to Chile on the political coattail of Mrs. Merwin's father, Reuben Wood. A lawyer in his middle twenties when he moved from Vermont to Cleveland, Ohio, in 1818, the direct, witty, and ambitious Wood had served successively as state senator, circuit court judge and justice of the state supreme court. Elected to the governorship of Ohio in 1850, he held that post until early 1853 when he resigned because of financial embarrassments. Meanwhile Wood's stature in the national councils of the Democratic party during the presidential election of 1852 prompted the claims that resulted in Secretary of State William L. Marcy's naming him consul for Valparaiso, Chile. That distant port, because of the exceedingly heavy volume of traffic it had enjoyed following the discovery of gold in California, was then considered a truly lucrative consular appointment. George B. Merwin, having served as his father-in-law's secretary during the gubernatorial years, was still at his side when tall, lean Reuben Wood embarked for South America.

The hardship and expense entailed by the five-week trip between New York and Valparaiso during the summer of 1853 heightened Consul Wood's anticipation of the fat fees awaiting him. Assuming his duties on 8 September, he immediately installed George B. Merwin as his secretary.

The disillusionment that set in as Wood surveyed the chaotic state of the records of his office quickly mounted. Food, clothing, and housing were unbelievably expensive. In his despatch of 2 October to Marcy, the new consul complained, "Rents are as high as in Broadway." That same day—less than one month after assuming office, he blurted out, "The receipts of the office have been *woefully overrated*." The Ohioan had discovered no pot of gold at the end of his Chilean rainbow. Indeed the traffic that had averaged twenty-five American ships per month at Valparaiso during the second half of 1850 had dwindled, three years later, to a mere half dozen vessels monthly.

The unhappy and impoverished "old Cuyahoga chief" won permission early in 1854 to return to Ohio, promising that "on my departure . . . the Consulate shall be placed in the hands of a competent American citizen." Politically it was best that he take one step at a time, so he did not mention the fact that the unidentified successor would be his son-in-law. On 28 July 1854, his departure imminent, Wood broke the word to Marcy, "I have this day appointed him [Merwin] Vice Consul." Upon reaching Washington on 5 December, Wood simultaneously submitted his own resignation and solicited the appointment of Merwin as his replacement. His claims upon his party were still considerable and Marcy speedily honored his request, appointing Merwin consul on 14 December 1854.

Methodical in executing the routine duties which he reported to his superiors in an elegant and delightfully legible hand, Merwin never faced any peculiarly significant problems in his office. A personal one, however, haunted him. His income from the consulship did not enable him to hire a clerk. In fact his household expenses and the rent he had to pay for his office combined to exceed his salary and fees.

While George worried about his finances and executed the protests, surveys, consular returns, registers of vessels, and all else related to his office, Loretta garnered the impressions which she embodied in *Three Years in Chile*.

Her book is a highly personal, yet strangely impersonal, account of life in Chile—personal in that one is always aware that he is sharing Chile through the eyes of one American woman, but impersonal in that the author never identifies herself or any member of her family. Much of that impersonal quality, beyond any reticence that might have characterized Mrs. Merwin, undoubtedly derived from the official position of her husband. Two decades earlier in Mexico Madame Calderón de la Barca had taken elaborate steps to protect the identity of her diplomat-husband but she had made her own identification easy by allowing her initials to appear on the title page of her *Life in Mexico*. Mrs. Merwin, on the other hand, not only protected the anonymity of the consul's-wife-turned-author on the title page, she also fortified that obscurity by allowing her publisher, Follett, Foster and Company, of New York City, to take out the copyright for her book. For the delayed publication of experiences concluded more than a half decade earlier, no precise explanation can be advanced. Perhaps delayed publication was but yet another diplomatic act of the consul's lady.

Other reasons also help to explain the reasonably detached rather than warmly involved picture of Chilean life found in *Three Years in Chile*. Beyond the linguistic limitation which made Mrs. Merwin more of an observer than participant and the diplomatic nicety which made her reluctant to tell all, both the ages of her children and the nature of her household tended to accentuate her detachment. The demands which two youngsters placed upon a dedicated mother naturally curtailed her involvement in Chilean society. In addition, the Wood-Merwin household, consisting as it did of four adult Americans—and Mrs. Wood tarried with the Merwins even after her husband's return to the States, had internal resources that made less necessary one's participation in outside society.

Such an insulated life abroad—of viewing rather than sharing in Chilean life—might have been catastrophic as the basis for a volume if the experience had been a brief one. In this instance, however, the repetition of the seasons, the holidays, the street scenes, the customs, etc. gave the author a more meaningful composite experience. What she might have shrugged off in 1853 was there for her wide-eyed wonderment in 1854, her comprehension in 1855, her delight in 1856. What might have been insufferably thin as reaction based on a onetime superficial experience comes through, instead, in rather impressive fashion as an aggregate experience. In places the structure of the book indicates that Mrs. Merwin either kept a diary or had made notes from time to time. The telescoping of time and the emphasis on topics which characterize *Three Years in Chile* strengthen the American woman's telling of her experiences.

In mid-September, 1856, overworked and underpaid Consul Merwin, complaining that his health had been impaired, sought permission to retire from his post. When no early reply came from Washington, he submitted his resignation to Minister D. A. Starkweather at Santiago. Merwin closed his brief consular career on December 31. Unwilling, perhaps unable, to pay $2200 passage for himself and his family by way of the Isthmus, as he had on their southbound trip, Merwin had arranged passage, for $1000, to Boston via Cape Horn. Wearied by the eleven-week voyage, the Merwins hurried to Ohio. The spring of 1857 found the Merwins and the Woods together again, at Rockport, near Cleveland. Their Chilean experiences of 1853–57 concluded, it but remained for Mrs. Merwin to record them for posterity.

Three Years in Chile revealed neither diplomatic nor social mysteries about Chile although the publication is itself associated with a minor one, for rumor has it that substantially the same text saw the light of day, likewise in 1863, under the title *Chile through American Spectacles*. Any spectacles that Mrs. Merwin may have worn were surely of limited magnification, for *Three Years in Chile* is a quiet and honest kind of assessment, the sort that could help her fellow citizens of the 1860's and the 1960's to a better awareness of Chilean life in mid-nineteenth-century years.

The editor's role, beyond the bio-bibliographical introduction, has included the following: a restructuring of the table of contents and the fashioning of chapter titles; some alterations in punctuation, especially the addition and deletion of commas; the modernization of some English spelling and the correction of some Spanish words; and the remedying of typographical errors of the edition of 1863. The text is complete.

The kind assistance of Director Meredith B. Colket, Jr. and Librarian Alene Lowe White of The Western Reserve Historical Society is gratefully acknowledged.

"The Oaks"   C. HARVEY GARDINER
Murphysboro, Illinois
February 1, 1966

THREE YEARS IN CHILE

I

From New York
to the Isthmus

We left New York on the 20th of July, and on the 28th of August entered the harbor of Valparaiso.

The voyage to Aspinwall was eventless, but full of interest and delight for us, to whom this seafaring experience was an entire novelty. On the 27th of July, we saw Cuba; and on the 28th we beheld the mountains of Jamaica, clothed from sea to summit with the perpetual verdure of sugar fields and coconut groves. The day was warm and bright, and we ran two hours along the coast, before putting into the bay of Port Royal—our vision feasted now with the glories of the land, and now with the beauty of the sparkling and joyous sea.

As you enter the bay, you see Port Royal on the right, crouching with low huts upon the level sands amid sheltering coconut trees; and at the head of the bay, Kingston, lying beneath a mountain that rises abruptly from the water, covered with dark masses of vegetation, and looking at first glance like a great thundercloud fallen heavily athwart the sight.

Here we stopped for coals, and before we made fast to the dock of the decaying city, the water about the steamer swarmed with unwonted life and activity: innumerable young Negroes clove the waves with their arms, and the air with their shouts, noisily besieging the passengers for money: "One dime, massa!" "One dime, missus!" When a coin was thrown to them, they dived through the transparent water and brought it up with unerring certainty, splashing, sputtering, blowing the brine from their faces, and greedily vociferating for more.

A plank walk was laid from the deck of the steamer to the coalyard, and about one hundred Negresses, scantily attired in ragged dresses that left bare the arms and neck and fell only to the knees, began the work of coaling. Each had a tub holding about a bushel, which she filled, and balanced on her head with one hand while she marched up the steep plank, keeping time to a chanted refrain. At the coalhole the tubs were emptied without being removed from the head by a sudden jerk of the neck and twist of the body; and the women passed off at the other end of the ship, in endless succession.

The hand of decay lies heavily upon Kingston. The narrow streets are filled with loose sand; the pavements are broken, and the houses almost universally dilapidated. Nevertheless, there were some handsome stores, where we found the merchants very polite, after we had struggled through the crowds of Negro boys who met us at every door and gateway, with vociferous invitations to enter. In the street, we saw not more than one white man to a hundred black ones, and the bitterest antipathy seemed to exist between the two races.

Disembarking at Aspinwall, on the 31st, with the usual scenes of bustle and confusion, we took the Panama Railroad for Barbacoa, twenty-three miles distant, and plunged suddenly into the heart of tropic scene. For a few miles from Aspinwall the road passes through a swamp on cribwork of logs, filled in with stone and earth, with the water on either hand thickly matted with aquatic plants. Traversing this swamp, we entered a great forest, magnif- icent with gigantic trees, all clambered with pendant, blossomy vines, and gorgeous with flowers of every hue. It was now the middle of the rainy season, when, in this tropical land, a few weeks suffice to clothe in vivid verdure every thing left undisturbed. In one place, near the road, stood an old piledriver, garlanded with luxuriant creep- ers; and in another, a dismantled locomotive was dimly discernible in a mass of green. Again, in harsh and ghastly contrast with this exuberant vegetable life, the end of a coffin protruded from a fallen bank, grimly wreathed with verdure.

After three hours' travel, we arrived at Barbacoa, and

quitting the cars, left behind us the civilization of the North and found ourselves not only in a tropical climate, amidst tropical scenery, but tropical mud, discomfort, and squalor.

Barbacoa stands on the bank of the Chagres River—a few bamboo huts, with a hotel distinguished by weather-boarding from the rest. We stopped at this hostelry for refreshments—taking our way from the cars to the house over a path of what seemed grass, but was really the delicate and beautiful sensitive plant, that shrank fearfully from the feet falling upon its tender leaves.

The place was full of Californians returning to the States, who gave us terrible accounts of the roads before us—for we were to take boats to Cruces, and thence struggle on with mules to Panama, *by mud.*

The railroad between Aspinwall and Panama has long been completed, and the perils and perplexities of the old-fashioned passage of the Isthmus are historical, rather than actual. I do not think, however, that their becoming

Portions and parcels of the dreadful past

has invested them with any tender hues of romance. They remain in my mind to this day a harsh reality of mud, deprivation, and affliction. I recount them with the sole consolation that for me they are past forever, and that no one hereafter will encounter them. Only, dear reader, as you are whirled along by steam over a passage memorable with direful struggles, bestow a sigh upon the hardships of pre-railroad travelers!

At the inn of Barbacoa we remained two hours, provisioning and bargaining for boats. When at last our arrangements were completed, we made our way through the town, and clambered down the steep muddy banks of the river to the water's edge, where we found about two hundred others, trying to embark, and mingling their tumult with the cries of the boatmen, who were shrieking loud demands of "*Hombre, aquí!*" on every hand. With great ado, a score of us succeeded in seating ourselves in a boat twenty feet in length—roofed, and with canvas at the sides, to be let down in case of rain. Our baggage was carried in the same boat, and served for seats; and then we had a captain, or steersman, and six boatmen, who propelled our craft keelboat fashion, by setting poles against the river bottom, and walking from the bow to the stern of the boat, on a narrow plank at either side. The greater part of the boats on the river were of this sort— some being distinguished by a red flag fluttering at the stern. The scene was rather pretty as a number of them pushed from the shore, into the middle of the river, with their gay bannerols waving, and freighted with men, women, and children in various costumes.

Our boatmen were great brawny fellows (naked but for a hat, and a piece of cloth girt about the loins), who accompanied every impulse of their poles with a deep sonorous grunt. We had not gone far, when we discovered that two of them were drunk; and presently one of them tumbled into the river. The current ran very rapidly, and we feared that the tipsy hombre was lost, when he came to the surface, and swimming after the boat, clambered in, only to make a second involuntary plunge, which sobered him.

On the banks of the river, which rose to a height of from four to twenty feet, we saw occasional patches of corn, and now and then a few cattle, and bamboo huts; but, for the most part, the view was shut off by impenetrable growths of trees, and interlacing vines and shrubs, through which a man could scarcely have hewn his way with an axe.

The afternoon was one of intense enjoyment to me; my eyes never wearied of the novel and ever-changing landscape, and the rich and beautiful forms of vegetation. At half past five we rounded to in front of Gorgona, a town then consisting of about forty bamboo huts, with a plaza and a populace enlivened by a mimic bullfight. Here our captain declared that his men must have something to eat, and the gentlemen of our party, going in search of food, returned with a dozen slices of ham and ten hard-boiled eggs—the only provisions to be had in all Gorgona. After an hour's delay we pushed off, and ascending the stream to the upper part of the town, our boatmen again ran the boat ashore, sprang out, struck a pole in the ground, made the boat fast, and, before we had time to think, plunged into the bushes and disappeared. It was now growing dark; no other boat was in sight; none of us could speak the language of the country; and all the tales of robbery and murder that we had ever heard, occurred to us, and some, at least, felt very uncomfortable. A party of the gentlemen went ashore to the alcalde, to learn, if possible, the reason of our detention, and were told that it was unlawful for any boat to navigate the river during the night. I was afterward told that a few months previous, a boat striking a snag was wrecked, and the passengers were drowned. The hombres were promptly arrested, tried, and shot for murder. On the following day, we ourselves found that it would have been impossible to proceed in a dark night, for the river was full of snags and sand bars.

All the boats that had left Barbacoa with us had been made fast along the shore at Gorgona, and discovering that we were not entirely alone, we set about rendering ourselves as comfortable as possible. A boatload of passengers, with the mails, tied up alongside, and the mail agent offered our gentlemen beds on the letter bags, and left us more room. From the other boat, we borrowed a candle and three matches, to be used in case of necessity. The night was very dark; a steady rain began to fall, and we crouched down upon our baggage, very hungry, weary, and miserable creatures. After awhile the children became uneasy, and we all suffered agonizing suspense while the attempt was made to light the candle. Two of the matches proved dead failures; but the third was a success. This excitement subsided, and I slept until roused by a crackling noise under my feet. On examination I found that I was trampling on my bonnet, which had dropped from my head. The comfortless night at last wore away, and at daylight our boatmen returned and put our boat in motion. At nine o'clock we reached Cruces, where the noisy scenes of the embarkation were repeated. Three men seized the three small children of our party, with the announcement of "Me picaninny Panama," and following their guidance, we ascended a slippery bank, and made our way between two rows of huts, through a street ankle-deep in mud and filth, swarming with pigs, poultry, donkeys, and children, to the St. Charles Hotel, where our martyrdom was consummated with a breakfast, which was the very abomination of indigestion.

II

CROSSING PANAMA

Our journey by water was now ended, but our troubles by land lay all before us. They began with the exchange of our traveling dresses for pantaloons, with short skirts and heavy boots. Thus equipped, with bonnets on our heads and coats on our backs, the question of sex was terribly vexed by our appearance. We all laughed, of course, at the ridiculous figures we cut; but we were rather shy of showing ourselves in the novel guise, until, going down stairs and rejoining the company, we found a great many other ladies in apparel far more astonishing than ours.

A Spanish gentleman who had accompanied us from New York, and who fortunately spoke English, made bargains for us with the muleteers. Some forty mules of different sizes, of different degrees of incapability, and all incredibly bruised and beaten, were paraded before the door of the hotel, where we selected the requisite number from the best, paying ten dollars for each mule, and eleven cents a pound for the transportation of our baggage. I had brought a sidesaddle from home, but when I put it on my mule, it left nothing of him visible but his head and tail; so I exchanged it for another mule. Each lady of our party selected as smart and sound an animal as possible, and then throwing her shawls upon the rude wooden saddle, mounted *en cavalier*, and sidled out of the crowd, in the direction of a green tree standing on the outskirts of the town, which was to be our rendezvous.

The usual arrangements for the transportation of the children had been made. Natives, for eight dollars apiece, had been hired to carry them; and they now shouldered their burdens and started off—the children screaming with the full power of their lungs. It is a sore trial for mothers to intrust their little ones to these great savages,

9

who, taking bypaths through the bushes, are often out of sight for hours. They usually carry the children safely, but there have been instances of drunkenness among them, when they left their charges in the road.

We did not quit our place of rendezvous without a number of amusing accidents. A French milliner of Panama, returning with goods from New York, was mounted on a spirited animal, that in spite of all her endearing caresses and appeals to his generosity, persisted in running away with her through the bushes, to the imminent peril of her neck, and was only prevailed upon to stop with great difficulty. Another lady lost her balance with the first movement of her mule, and dashed wildly from her perch into the mud. She was not hurt, and as this was her first experience on muleback, she repeated the same interesting performance five times during the day. One of the gentlemen went back to the hotel for something that had been left, and his mule absolutely refused to set forth again. At length our friend made his appearance, the mule disputing every inch of the ground, with one native tugging at the bridle, another pushing in the rear, and the rider indiscriminately belaboring all parts of his body. It is only after a long acquaintance with this animal that one understands the term *mulish* in all its profound significance.

At our rendezvous a number of pack mules were collected, each laden with two hundred and fifty pounds, in two packages, piled high on either side. They carry enormous trunks in this way; but sometimes small and feeble animals stagger and fall beneath their burdens, and in their frantic efforts to rise, roll backward and forward two or three times, before regaining their feet. Leaving our station tree, we plunged at once into yellow clay two feet deep, and the mules, knowing too well the hardships before them, at first refused to proceed, and it required the most desperate exertions to put them in motion. When once in motion, however, these creatures, if nature held out, would be perpetual motions. It is as hard to stop them as to start them.

It was now noon. We started single file—first through mud, then through bushes, then into narrow defiles from three to twenty feet deep, where two mules could not pass, and where constant care alone preserved our feet from being bruised against the rocks on either side. At times we turned angles so sharp, that we could not see ten feet ahead; emerging upon a short level, to commence so steep an ascent that we had to clasp our mules' necks, to keep from sliding off backward; a moment for breath, and then down, down through gorges of loose rocks and water where foothold seemed impossible. But giving our mules their heads, they put their noses to the ground to ascertain if there was safe footing, then put down one cautious foot after the other, and safely accomplished the descent, never stumbling once. Now and then we came to the trunk of a tree across our path, three feet in diameter, but the mules surmounted this obstacle without trouble. All these exercises were amusingly varied by the passage of mud, and mudholes filled with loose stones, in which the traveler floundered desperately, till the mule sank beneath him, and it only remained for him to dismount, and drag out his beast.

We had not seen the children now since we started; but on arriving at a wayside hut, we found them at play, perfectly safe and happy. These huts are merely thatched roofs sustained by four posts. The residents usually supplied travelers with refreshments, such as poor claret, ham, yams, and bread.

Although we had left Cruces too late in the day to expect to reach Panama that night, we determined to push on as far as possible. As twilight approached, however, we began to look anxiously for some place to pass the night. In most parts of the United States, we could have camped out for the night, but here every inch of ground, except the narrow footway, was covered with an impenetrable mass of trees and plants, that would have baffled all attempts at a bivouac. We paused a moment in front of a hut on the summit of a hill, but were decided to move on by the aspect of a crowd of unwholesome and forbidding natives about the door. After two miles' farther travel, we came in sight of another house, likewise set on a hill, and here our complete exhaustion determined us to remain. It was already growing dark, and between us and our goal stretched a vast sea of mud; our hearts sunk, and the beasts that we bestrode sunk too. On our right, an unfortunate mule had been mired, and had died standing, and now with a plumptitude of body that he had never known in life, glared horribly at us out of his dead eyes; in front of us, three pack mules had fallen, and in their efforts, rolled over and over, until they were covered and blinded with mud, while their inhuman drivers stood over them, inciting them to new exertions with kicks, blows and yells. I felt a calm conviction that we were to be swallowed up in this miry sea; but not to attempt the passage, seemed equally fatal. So we plunged in, and after prodigious and incredible efforts, our reeking mules dragged us to the door of the house, where we women, more dead than alive, were lifted off—to find the children safe, and five companions in misfortune, awaiting us.

This house, which bore the cruelly significant name of the Elephant Hotel, was a large inclosure of bamboo poles, driven closely together into the earth, and fastened at the top, with withes of bark, roofed with canvas, open at the gable ends, and divided into kitchen, dining-room, and two dormitories. In one of these latter, which was very large, was a row of beds: that is, pieces of sacking fastened to upright poles, and rising one above the other, in three tiers, to the roof. Beside these beds there were some movable cots. On a large piece of canvas stretched across an opening in front of the hotel, the symbolic animal from which the house was named, was rudely sketched in outline.

After a passable supper of mutton, beans, bread and coffee, we retired—the women replacing their muddy garments with dry dresses; and the wretched gentlemen of our party lying down in their muddy clothes—afraid to remove even their boots, lest they should refuse to "go on" in the morning. We used our shawls for bedding, and in this room we all slept, men, women, children, and muleteers. Long before this, we had found that necessity knows no law.

The night was cold and damp, the wind whistled through the crevices of the Elephant, our covering was insufficient, and so, within eight degrees of the equator, we shivered till daylight, when we were roused from the drowsy torpor into which we had fallen by the screams of myriads of parrots, and rose—weary, wretched and sore— breakfasted, and made ready for another day of horrors.

III

Panama City

We had yet a ride of thirteen miles before us. As we set forth, the first gentleman who mounted stuck fast in the mud, within ten feet of the door, and was obliged to dismount before the mule could extricate himself.

Our path now lay through uplands, where we mounted steep acclivities and threaded dark ravines, under lofty, overarching trees, between the boughs of which the deep azure of the sky was dimly visible. In these rocky hills, the muleteer, as he approaches the entrance of each of the narrow gorges, utters a shrill cry to know if there are others in the passage; receiving no response, he proceeds. The small rapid streams became more numerous, and the country more hilly, with a delightful vista opening here and there, of sky, and trees, and water. Some of the acclivities have been traveled so many years, that the mules have worn, with their hoofs, footholds in the solid rock more than twelve inches in depth. Occasionally, we passed over several rods together of the paved road said to have been constructed by the buccaneers.

Of the inhabitants of the country, we saw more women than men. The dress of the former usually consisted of a flounced muslin or calico gown, low in the neck, with a white cape ruffled or trimmed with lace, leaving the shoulders and arms entirely bare. They lounged about the doors of their huts, and sat on low stools, with their wide skirts spread upon the ground. The men wore nothing but a shirt, though occasionally we met one with an unusually keen sense of the proprieties, who carried a pair of pantaloons on his shoulder, to be put on before entering the city.

The road, as we neared Panama, grew worse and worse, and we were fearfully fatigued, while the children's

faces were blistered by the sun, and their limbs galled by
the hot hands of the men who carried them. At last, plod-
ding wearily on, we climbed a little eminence, and caught
a glimpse, in the distance, of the white spires of Panama,
and the blue waters of the Pacific, the city and the ocean,
the sight of which had gladdened so many weary hearts,
in our own time, and in the centuries past. We were met
here by several men on horseback, who proclaimed to us
the virtues and advantages of the different hotels, for
which they were agents; but our hearts were won by a
magnificently mounted gentleman, who announced himself as the proprietor of the American Hotel, and gave us
the splendid assurance that his house was not only the best
in the city, in all respects, but added the luxury of fine
baths to its other comforts. Passing between rows of squalid
huts, inclosed with cactus, and on by the ruins of an old
church, with its obelisks of masonry, crosses and images,
we crossed several stone bridges, and entered at the eastern
gate of Panama, and all bowed with fatigue, and dripping
with mud, arrived at the portal of the American Hotel.
The idea of baths, and consequent cleanliness, had taken
such firm hold in our diseased imaginations, that we had
hardly entered the room assigned to us, before we demanded them. In compliance with our request, a native,
with the most imposing dignity, and an air of self-satisfac-
tion that plainly demanded, "What more could you
desire?" brought us a half barrel of water, and set it down
in the middle of the floor.

This hotel, in the palmy days of Panama, was the
Bishop's palace. It is a large three-story house, built of
bricks brought from Spain, and roofed with tile. The two
upper stories are surrounded with corridors, on which all
the doors open. The building is floored throughout with
square tile.

The weather was very hot and rainy; one moment the
sun shone fiercely, and the next, the rain flooded the
streets, that smoked like a vapor bath when the sun shone
again. The housetops, the edges of the pavements, and

every place not constantly trodden upon, teemed with vegetation, plants and mosses, all alive with lizards. We were cautioned to look into our shoes before putting them on in the morning, lest there should be scorpions in them, and always remembered the caution—just after tying them.

To describe Panama to American readers, would be like describing New York or Boston, or any other city with which we are familiar. During our brief sojourn we "did" its most interesting features—the cathedral, built of brick, and decorated within in the worst style—where we saw among other figures that of the Virgin habited in a short tarlatan dress, and looking like a ballet dancer; the promenade on the seawall, with its dismounted guns, overlooking the bay and islands; the innumerable bells of the churches, all cracked, and beaten with hammers instead of being run. The city is walled; the streets are narrow; and the houses of brick, whitewashed, with the second story projecting over the sidewalks; they are all roofed and floored with tile.

IV

Coasting South America

On the 7th of August, we put to sea once more, on board the iron steamer "Bolivia," with every prospect of a pleasant voyage. On the 10th, we crossed the equatorial line, wearing our blanket shawls all day, and sitting close to the chimneys to keep warm. On the 11th, we ran up the Guayaquil River, in Ecuador, and anchored at the city of the same name, forty miles from the sea. The river is a broad, noble stream, between one and two miles wide. Its banks are clothed with a dense forest of stately trees, among which I noticed the ebony tree, covered with yellow blossoms.

The city of Guayaquil looks well from the anchorage, but on landing, we found it like all other Spanish-American cities. The streets are narrow, and the houses are built of wood framed into posts of *lignum vitæ*, planted firmly in the ground. This mode of building has been found by experience to be the most secure against injury by earthquakes, as the houses will shake without falling. The heat was excessive. In the market we found most of our summer vegetables, and many tropical vegetables besides. The cacao bean, from which chocolate is made, forms one of the principal exports. Guayaquil is also the great depot for Panama hats, eight hundred thousand dollars worth being sold annually. The grass of which they are made, is found chiefly in the neighboring province of San Cristóbal. They can be braided only in the night or early morning, as the heat in the daytime renders the grass brittle. It takes a native about three months to braid one of the finest quality, and I saw some hats which looked like fine linen, and were valued at fifty dollars apiece, even here.

At Guayaquil we took on a supply of water, which

17

was furnished in a manner peculiar to the country. An immense raft, made of balsa logs (a light, porous wood), came alongside; its whole space (except one corner occupied by a little thatched hut) covered by carrot-shaped earthen jars, containing each about eighteen gallons of water. These jars were brought one by one, and emptied into the steamer's tanks.

We left the city at four the same afternoon, and rapidly descended the river, with steam and tide. At the mouth of the Guayaquil lies the island of Pima, on which Pizarro landed before invading Peru. On the morning of the 13th, we passed Tumbez, the first point on the Peruvian coast, and at one o'clock stood off Cape Blanco, a bold, sandy promontory, with the breakers dashing high upon it; at five we were abreast of Cape Perina, the most westerly point of South America, and at nine we anchored in Paita Bay. The town is a cluster of miserable bamboo huts containing about fifteen hundred souls, of whom the greater part are Indians. Water is brought thither a distance of twenty-five miles, on the backs of mules, and not a blade of grass grows in all the barren land about; all vegetables are brought from Pima, a fertile valley, twenty miles from Paita. These vegetables, and the fruits, are of good quality. There are two kinds of sweet potatoes—the white and purple, which are large, round, and much sweeter than those of the United States. Here they have also yellow Irish potatoes, which are excellent, but which degenerate in quality elsewhere, after the first crop. The fruits are apples, peaches, lemons (sweet and sour), melons, pomegrantes, cherimoyas, granadillas, paltas, and many others of intertropical growth. The sweet lemon was round, and to me was quite tasteless. The cherimoya is considered the best fruit of South America. The tree is from fifteen to twenty feet in height, and is of slow growth. The blossoms are small, white and fragrant. The fruit is heart-shaped, and grows from two to five inches in diameter—I have seen some specimens measuring over six inches. When ripe, the skin is tough, not very thick,

brownish-yellow in color, and covered with a scaly network. The pulp is something of the consistence of baked
custard, yellow-white, with a number of brown seeds in
the center. The flavor of the cherimoya has been likened
to that of strawberries and cream, but this I think an exag-
geration. Varieties differ as widely in taste as apples. The
palta (sometimes called alligator pear by foreigners)
grows upon a tall, slender tree, and is of a brownish-green
color, about as large as a goose egg, and pear-shaped. The
pulp is greenish-yellow, and melts upon the tongue like
marrow. Some persons become exceedingly fond of it,
but the taste was always very offensive to me. The
granadilla is the fruit of a species of the passionflower; it
is egg-shaped, with a thick, reddish-yellow skin; the pulp,
which is pleasantly acid, is filled with numerous seeds.

Early on the morning of the 18th we arrived at Callao, another Peruvian town—a dreary, uninviting place,
with flat, one-story houses, built of canes, and plastered
on the outside. The narrow streets intersect at right angles,
and are filled almost to suffocation with dirt and dust,
which the fine winter mists (for it never rains here) convert
into impassable mire.

Old Callao, which stood farther out on the point than
the present town, was destroyed by an earthquake and the
sea, in 1746, when four thousand lives were lost, and many
of the vessels in the harbor were borne far inland by the
invading ocean. Some of the ruins of the devoted city are
still visible.

The new town wears an air of almost northern bustle
and activity. Uninjured by the skies of this rainless clime,
vast piles of wheat (containing from ten to fifteen thousand
bushels) lie uncovered upon the mole; and the streets are
thronged by water carriers, venders of fruits and dulces
(the generic name in Spanish for sweetmeats), sailors,
boatmen, and troops of freight donkeys; so that it was
only with great dexterity and alertness that we made our
way through the confusion, redolent with all the smells
of garlic-fed squalor.

There is a railroad between Callao and Lima (a distance of six miles), on which trains make half-hourly trips. This road is owned by three persons, whose daily income from it is about fifteen thousand dollars.

Aquatic birds, pelicans, boobies, gulls, Cape pigeons, and others, abounded in such numbers that they fairly darkened the air, flying, screaming, and darting for fish. The pelican diverted us greatly. Plunging into the sea, he would emerge with his great pouch full of fish—usually the tails of three or four protruding—when another kind of bird which was hovering in wait, gave chase, and seldom failed in snatching part of the pelican's booty. I had often marveled at the immense deposits of guano, but after seeing the myriads of birds on this coast, I ceased to wonder. It is a fine of twenty-five dollars to kill one of these birds, or even to discharge a gun in Callao Bay, or at the Chincha Islands.

At two o'clock we left our steamer, and taking passage on a much larger and better one, put to sea again. I deeply regretted our inability to visit Lima, the city of so many historic associations, and the burial place of Pizarro, whose remains are still to be seen underneath the lofty altar of the great cathedral.

By the morning of the 19th we had made the port of Pisco—a pretty town near a valley, teeming with vegetation, where the best oranges on the Pacific coast are grown. They are large, luscious, and cheap—we bought three hundred for two dollars.

Large quantities of wine and rum are made here, and sent to Callao and other ports along the coast. They distill also a pure aromatic liquor from the Italian grape, called Italia de Pisco. It is put up in carrot-shaped earthen jars, each holding about three gallons—and is much esteemed by connoisseurs of good liquor—making, it is said, a delicious punch.

The Chincha Islands, three in number, lie ten miles off in a northwestern direction from Pisco. Not a green thing grows on all their vast extent and depth of fertilizing ano, which restores life and vigor to so many thousands exhausted acres.

Passing out of the bay to the south, our attention was rested by a curiously shaped cross, apparently made of ht-colored stones, set in the sloping rock of the cliff, and me two hundred feet from top to bottom. It commem- ates an affair between the Spaniards and Indians in the d times, and is a place of annual solemnities with the vout, led thither by the priests.

V

More Ports
Quickly Glimpsed

At seven o'clock on the morning of the 22nd, we anchored in the Bay of Arica. The present town lies close to the beach, at the foot of a bluff. As seen from the steamer it looked very prettily; but its charms did not stand the test of a sultry walk through narrow, dusty streets, in the glare of whitewashed walls. A small stream from the valley of Azapa supplies the inhabitants and shipping with drinking water.

Enclosed, at a little distance from the town, is a burial ground of the ancient Peruvians, but most of the graves have been violated by foreigners, and sacrilegious curiosity has spared few of the bodies, which the dry air and nitrous soil preserved for centuries.

Arica has been twice almost destroyed by earthquakes, attacked twice by buccaneers, and once nearly desolated by revolutionary struggles.

Vegetables, fruits, and even flowers are largely exported. The dealers are women, one of whom accompanied us to Valparaiso, trading at every port. The women of this coast are much superior to the men in point of intellect, activity, and what we should call go-ahead-ativeness. The people are of all shades of color, from dark brown to white, with high cheekbones, large mouths, and coarse, black hair. For the most part they are excessively ugly. The men are dressed as with us, but they wear, instead of a coat, the poncho, which is a square blanket, with a slit in the center, through which to thrust the head—varying in color and quality, according to the taste and wealth of the wearer. It is the distinguishing mark of the peon of the country. The hats are of different styles—cheap Panama, little conical hats of blue felt, and straw. The women wear calicoes, muslins, and worsted plaids, usually of gay colors—with a shawl doubled square, and one end thrown over the left shoulder. The hair hangs in heavy braids down the back. If by chance the shawl slips off, the gaping dress—never fastened at the bottom of the waist—reveals the underclothing. This slovenliness is characteristic of the women of all classes, in a greater or less degree.

On the 25th we arrived at Iquique. A more desolate, forlorn-looking place, could not be imagined. It lies at the base of a rocky wall more than two hundred feet in height, and there is not a drop of fresh water, nor a spear of living green for thirty miles round about. Saltpeter, the only export of much value, is brought from the mines in the mountains, a distance of twelve leagues. The vein is three feet thick, extending, around the margin of a great plain, a hundred miles. I was told that the mules employed in carrying the saltpeter, have no food nor drink from the time they leave the mines till their return, on the third day. There are extensive and rich silver mines in the vicinity of this place, which were formerly wrought by the Spanish government, but were filled up during the revolution, and have remained in that condition ever since.

Drinking water is distilled from sea water, or brought forty miles in boats from the river Pisaqua. We saw here, and at no other port, a curious kind of boat (or bolsa, as the natives call it), constructed of two sealskins, made airtight, lashed side by side and inflated—the boatman, or bolsero, sitting in the middle, on a little platform of canes or rushes, using a double-bladed oar, with which, dipping first on one side and then on the other, he propelled his craft with great velocity. These boats are safe, and will go through a surf in which no other boat could live.

We made Cobija, another of these desert coast towns, on the 24th. This is the only seaport of Bolivia. In the vicinity are valuable copper mines, of which the products are shipped at Catica and Algodones. The inhabitants seized eagerly upon the garden stuff of our Arica traders, and in a few moments half the people of Cobija, I believe, were chewing sugar cane.

On the following day we stopped at Caldera, a tow
of three years' growth, containing 1700 inhabitants, ar
the port for the city of Copiapó. It was laid out by a
American, and owes its growth wholly to Yankee ente
prise. The harbor is a fine one, and has the only dock on tl
whole coast. A railroad had just been finished from Ca
dera to Copiapó (fifty miles), for bringing down silver ar
copper, in the ores and in bars. We took on board eight
six bars of silver, each one of which was valued at twent
five hundred dollars. Caldera is utterly destitute of vegeta
tion and fresh water—sea water being distilled for drin.
ing and the engines.

VI

Valparaiso—A Panorama

It was the morning of the 28th, when we entered the bay
of Valparaiso. We rose early, packed our trunks, and then
went on deck, eager for the first glimpse of that terrestrial
paradise, in whose delicious climate of perpetual sunshine,
amid orange groves filled with birds of gorgeous plumage,
we were to live without care and without effort. We had
some such fond dream of Chilean existence, as nearly
every one has of southern lands, but it was soon dispelled.
The morn was cool and dark, and we shivered under our
heavy shawls, while the promised land remained invisible
until we entered the port, and then only showed itself very
vaguely. After while we beheld the city, lying upon the
shore, and hanging upon the slopes of the verdant hills—
for it was now near the close of the rainy season, and all the
land was vividly green.

Crowds of boats flocked toward our steamer, the
boatmen clamoring in Spanish, and making an incredible
uproar; but none were allowed to come alongside until
the captain of the port had visited the steamer, as is the
custom with all vessels entering the harbor. He ascertains
their nationality, the number of their passengers, and the
nature of their cargoes, and the name of the last port from
which they sailed—to be entered upon the books of the
Bolsa, or Merchant's Exchange.

Selecting one boat for ourselves and another for our
baggage, we made our way to shore, half-bewildered with
strange sights and sounds. A gentleman kindly accompanied us to the Hotel Aubrey (one of the best in the city),
where we found comfortable rooms, and made very satis-
factory experiment of the cuisine in an immediate breakfast. The hotel, three stories in height, is built against a
perpendicular wall of rock, towering up three times as

25

high as the building, with cactus and many flowering plants growing from the crevices.

The history of the port of Valparaiso runs back to 1543, but when the city was founded is uncertain. During the first days of our residence, we walked every morning, without success in our attempts to form definite ideas of the shape of the place. The main part of the city is built on a narrow strip of land, three miles long, and not of the same width anywhere for ten rods together, which terminates at the west in a bold, rocky promontory several hundred feet in height, and on the east by a rocky bluff. Then abruptly hills rise to a height of two hundred feet, with more or less level ground beyond, for nearly half a mile, where they tower up thirteen hundred feet. These hills are broken with numerous quebradas (ravines), radiating from the shore. One spur called Cape Horn, projecting further than the others, originally extended to the water, almost dividing the city in half, and only to be passed at low tide, but this has been blasted and cut away, until now a street, with a row of houses on either side, lies at its base.

The eastern quarter of the city (called the Almendral, from a grove of almond trees once planted there by Augustine monks) is built on ground made by human labor and the torrents washing the sand from the hills. The western part, called El Puerto, or the port, is clustered about the mole; it is chiefly commercial, and nearly all the residents are foreigners. Streets follow the windings of the principal ravines to the summits of the hills, and are passable to no other vehicle but the birlocho—a sort of gig rather heavier than that in use with us.

There are three plazas in Valparaiso—Victoria, del Orden, and Municipalidad. The Victoria plaza only is of considerable size. On one side of it fronts the church San Augustín, and on the other stands the theater—a handsome building, capable of seating two thousand persons.

Houses are built along the ravines and on the hilltops, and thrust cornerwise and sidewise into the hill slopes, partially supported by rude foundations of earth and rock, or resting on posts, with the appearance of being on stilts. The hills are the favorite resort of the sailors, and several have nautical names—as the Maintop, Mizzentop and Foretop. Cerro Alegre is the pleasantest of all. It is occupied entirely by foreigners, and every house has its little inclosure of choice plants—a luxury purchased at considerable expense in this barren place, where water for irrigation must be bought six months of the year.

There are six Catholic churches in the city. The churches of Matriz, San Augustín and Merced are the principal ones, of which the latter only is finished. Most of the dwelling houses, particularly in the Almendral, are one story in height, built of adobes, with patios, white-washed and roofed with tile. The adobes are bricks made of a mixture of clay and straw, and dried in the sun. They are eighteen inches long, nine wide, and three thick. The patio is a court or yard inclosed by the walls of the house. The tile roofing is made of half cylinders of pottery, about eighteen inches long by eight in diameter. The roof is first prepared by boarding; it is then coated with mud, and the tiles are laid in courses, the concave side up, from the ridge to the eaves, the upper tiles lapping over the under, with other courses laid convex upon the edges, and a row forming the ridge. They are of a reddish-brown color, and give rather a pleasing effect to the city roofs.

The houses of more than one story are chiefly to be found in the port. They are made of wood framed carefully together, lathed inside and outside with bamboo, and plastered. The bamboo is brought from Guayaquil— large sticks, forty feet long by eight inches in diameter, are split and make excellent lathing. All buildings have the first-story windows defended by iron bars, often wrought in fanciful devices, but all unpleasantly suggesting prison grates.

Since the buildings are made less of adobe and more of wood, the injuries from earthquakes in Valparaiso are not so serious as formerly; a wooden house is flexible, and

will vibrate a great deal without falling. A balcony p
jects from the upper story of each house, over the sidewa
and the first floor is commonly used for warerooms, stor
offices, etc., while the dwellings are in the upper part
the building.

The city is adorned with magnificent stores, c
stantly importing from Europe, and furnishing eve
article of use or luxury that can be required. The sh
windows dazzle the eye with their rich displays of lac
silks, and diamonds. There are silks made expressly
the South American market, and I have never seen su
splendid fabrics anywhere else. An old resident who
moved to New York a few months since sent back to V
paraiso to buy dresses for his daughter.

In the Almendral there is a fine public garden, fill
with rare flowering plants, with broad walks sheltered
trellises of grapevines—which is open at all times to vi
tors. Twice a week, during the summer season (Sund
and Wednesday evenings), the promenaders are enliven
by music. The garden is then a great resort for the élite
Valparaiso.

The streets are full of strange sights to us. Here in t
Plaza Municipalidad are groups of women selling shoes
a piece of cloth or old carpet thrown upon the ground n
the curb-stone, and the vendor sitting on a low stool, w
her stock of trade arranged in the interior of a large, sh
low basket before her. She has for sale men's and bo
coarse leather shoes, and women's gaiters of all colors. S
sits here the whole day long, shifting her stool to keep c
of the sun, and now and then resigning it to the purchas
who wishes to try on a shoe.

Clattering along through the street comes the wa
carrier—a little donkey with a wooden frame on eith
side, sustaining a keg which holds about eight gallons
water. The donkey has no bridle, but a man or boy follo
him. He stops at your door, and if you live up stairs, t
man ascends with one keg at a time, and pours it into yo
water barrel. If you live on the first floor, the donkey

driven into the patio. After the water is delivered and the kegs replaced, the man mounts so far back upon the donkey's hind quarters that it is hard to tell which animal the tail belongs to—and away they go on a hard trot for a new supply, the kegs banging in their frames, and the rider belaboring the donkey over either ear, according as he wants him to turn to the right or left.

After the water carrier comes the bread man. All the bread supplied from public bakeries is of excellent quality. Men on mules traverse the city, bringing it to the people's doors every morning. They are equipped with two panniers, nearly a foot square, made of hide, and often carry a basket or bag full of bread on top of these; the rider sits on the mule's shoulders, and the establishment occupies nearly the whole width of the narrow street.

The milkman carries his milk in two small tin cans, suspended on either side of his mule, and comes so far and rides so fast, that the fluid is often half-churned when you get it.

The laundress bringing your washed clothes, fetches them on her back—passing her hand over her shoulder, grasping the bands, and holding the garments at full length that they may not be wrinkled.

The hotels here are all conducted on the French plan —breakfast from eight to twelve, and dinner at five, with no other regular meal, though you can have lunch or tea if you order it. At the table d'hôte gentlemen smoke between the courses, and at intervals along the table are placed little three-legged metal cups, containing coals of fire by which to light the cigarritos. One admirable feature in the hotel cuisine is, that whether you have coffee, tea, or chocolate for breakfast, it is made for you alone, and brought in a small pot, with a pitcher of hot milk and a dish of sugar. In this way you get it fresh, and not as we do at our large American hotels, where it is made in quantity, and where you only know the beverage by its color.

As this is the land of earthquakes, we began life in it, with daily expectations of the temblor—fearfully curious about our sensations. Our first experience was somewhat ludicrous. We had dined out, and about nine o'clock in the evening, while the gentlemen were still at table, we in the parlor were discussing the subject of earthquakes, and our hostess remarked, "I always run into the street," and then sprang suddenly from the sofa, exclaiming—"There is one now! Ladies, there is the door," and flew to the nursery to secure her little ones—leaving us standing transfixed with terror, staring at each other, utterly ignorant (for it was the first time we had been in the house) which door opened into the street. I only remember groping my way through a dimly lighted hall, and lifting my feet as if I were walking the deck of a rolling ship. This was so slight a shock that we should never have noticed it ourselves.

It was now the close of winter, and very cool, so that until nine in the morning, and after four in the afternoon, we suffered excessively even with thick shawls on. There were no fires in the house, and we ordered a brasero, a brass pan on three legs, and filled with charcoal, which is lighted and placed in the open air until well burned, when it is brought into the room. We always had headache from it.

I went to market soon after our arrival in Valparaiso. The market house consists of two or three large rooms crowded with all sorts of things in season, piled up in baskets or on the floor—and the place swarming with filthy people. Every thing was so fearfully dirty, that I almost concluded to fast during my residence in Chile. There were in market, green peas, beans, lettuce, radishes, squashes, turnips, and potatoes, all of good quality; and turkeys, chickens, partridges, very good beef, poor mutton and veal, and various kinds of scale and shellfish.

After much earnest search for a house, we finally decided to rent the house and purchase the furniture of an American engineer who had been in the employment of the Chilean government three or four years, and was now going home. In Valparaiso we found a small, but pleasant society of Americans, our nation being less numerously represented there than either the English, Germans, or French. There are two Protestant places of worship in the city—that of the Congregationalists, and that of the Church of England, under the patronage of the British Consul.

With the natives, Sunday, so sacred with us, is a grand gala day, and every Sabbath morning the streets are gay with military and music, pleasure parties starting to the country, and people hurrying from mass—the fine lady to finish the day at the opera, and the peasant to crown her devotions at the fandango.

VII

One Household
and Two Cemeteries

NOVEMBER. We took possession of our house on the 1st of October, and occupy the whole upper story. Ours is like most other two-story houses here. It has a kitchen, dining room, parlor, and seven bedrooms. The dining room is in the middle of the house, and is lighted by two small windows in the roof. All the other rooms open upon a corridor, which extends around three sides of the building. The kitchen is very small, with a curious brick range in the center. The walls and fixtures are all as black as a chimney flue, and utterly revolting to the spirit of Yankee housekeeping within me. We have the whole establishment at a rent of $800 per annum.

We engaged a cook and retained our predecessor's manservant, neither of whom spoke one word of English, while we were equally ignorant of Spanish. We took possession in the morning, and found no cook. The dinner hour came, and there was no dinner. We had nothing in the house but some groceries and bread, and could buy nothing because we could not speak the language of traffic, and even if we had had plenty of provisions, we could have cooked nothing on that incomprehensible range! So the gentlemen went back to the hotel and breakfasted, while we satisfied our appetites upon bread and butter.

A friend called during the evening, and suggested, that until we could procure a cook, we should have our meals brought us from a café. This is quite a common custom, I find. You have a set of tins made, fitting one into the other, with a wire passing through rings at the side. The bottom tin contains coals, and the different meals and vegetables are placed in the successive tins above. At dinner-time one may see men rushing through the streets in every direction, with these strings of dishes, varying in length, according to the magnitude of the purchaser's dinner.

We lived in this way for a week, receiving applications without number from cooks; and finally hired one who came well recommended—an old woman of about sixty. She is to have eight dollars a month for cooking two meals a day, washing the greater part of the dishes, and going to market for us. She sleeps in her own house. It is droll to see me in the evening approach my cook to give instructions about marketing—bearing money in one hand and a dictionary in the other. I have learned the pronunciation of the language, which is not difficult, and I dispense entirely with verbs. The brief dialogue is something in this manner:

I—María, beefsteak, papas, huevos (potatoes, eggs).

María (invariably)—Bueno, señorita (very good, Miss).

The manservant (majordomo, he is magnificently styled here) is our chambermaid, takes charge of the dining room, and waits at table.

We have one street staircase up which every thing is brought. The first thing I hear in the morning is the clatter upon the steps of the water carrier, who brings us two kegs of water daily, for which he receives two dollars and a half a month; then the bread man, whom we pay half a dollar daily for what our family of seven and two servants consume. (In addition to meats and vegetables from our table, servants are entitled to one pound of good brown sugar a week, and three cents' worth of bread a day. Butter is never allowed them.) Next comes the milkman with half a pint for six cents. Lastly the cook arrives with the marketing, and fuel with which to cook it.

This is a novel way of living from hand-to-mouth, and I always have an impression that some day we shall be left destitute. It is, however, very easy for housekeepers, for no bread is made in the house, and no washing is done at home. Our laundress comes on Monday, takes away our soiled linen, and brings the clean. But one must keep a close account of every article to guard against theft. At first, of course, we had a great deal of trouble, and the servants managed matters pretty much in their own way.

I never so keenly felt my ignorance of language, as the other evening when a Chileno with his family called to pay their respects, and we sat mutely staring at each other —eager to talk, and our heads, no doubt, full of bright ideas, while we were obliged to confine our conversation to saying "Buenas noches" (good night). I was desperate, and studied Spanish next morning with prodigious vigor.

Fires are not allowed in the port for other than cooking purposes, except by special permission of the Intendente. The natives use the brasero occasionally on cool evenings, but foreigners have introduced a few Yankee coal stoves, placing them usually in the dining room, and projecting the pipe through the window. There is one in our house arranged as Mr. C. left it, in this manner, and one rainy day I attempted to light a fire in it. As the volume of smoke poured out of the window, a policeman came hurrying up the stairs and into the room, vociferating Spanish. I did not understand a word, though I knew the purport of his visit; so I worked away at my fire, and replied in English that I was cold, and that the fire would soon burn. He expostulated in Spanish, and I rejoined again in English, and being a woman, out-talked him, and he went off. In a few moments more, with his spurs and sword clattering along the corridor, came an officer of police, upon whom I tried the measures so effectual with his subordinate, and each of us talked at the other in the wildest and most incomprehensible manner. At last, in sheer desperation, he ended the matter by tearing the fire to pieces with his hands.

We walk daily. All but the principal streets are narrow, filthy, and crowded with men, women, children, donkeys, and dogs, while the dust swarms with fleas. As you pass along through the poorer quarters, you notice in the doorways, picturesque family groups of people, making those interesting examinations of each others' heads, which, among the infested of some other lands, are usually conducted in private. Here, however, the strongest light is sought.

Places of resort with us are the Catholic and Protestant cemeteries, which are situated on the summit of one of the hills, and are both surrounded with adobe walls, tastefully ornamented with plants and trees. These cemeteries are separated by a narrow lane. That of the Catholics is on the crest of the hill overlooking the bay; that of the Protestants in the rear of the other. Each has a chapel to which it is the custom to bring the dead at midnight, and lock them up, performing the funeral services at an appointed hour the next day.

In the Catholic grounds are some fine monuments, of which the most beautiful was erected by the Municipality of Valparaiso, to the memory of Portales, perhaps the most brilliant statesman Chile has produced. It is a shaft of pure white marble, with a pointed cap, which has been half turned round by earthquakes. The monument, which contains the heart of the deceased patriot, is appropriately inscribed.

There are vaults and tombs to be used permanently by those who can pay for them, but other graves are rented for one year, at the expiration of which time the bodies are dug up, the bones thrown in a deep pit, and the coffins burned. For the wretched poor, those who have no money at all, excavations of fifteen or twenty feet square, and ten or twelve deep, are made, into which the bodies, wrapped in cloth, are thrown, layer upon layer, with earth over each, until the whole space is filled. It is then smoothed over, and another pit is prepared.

In the middle of the Catholic cemetery stands an octagonal wall of masonry, ten feet in diameter by twelve in height, and surmounted by an iron railing—this incloses a deep pit where the bones are heaped together. On my first visit, a ladder was standing against the wall, and I saw, with an indescribable horror, the leg of a skeleton dangling over the railing.

We are not satisfied with the location of our house, from which nothing is to be seen but filthy people, donkeys, dogs, and sailors' boardinghouses.

The other day I noticed in the street a donkey load that excited my curiosity. It consisted of dirty, yellow lumps of something, which on inquiry proved to be tallow from the country, put up, as is the custom, in the stomachs of cattle. Our butter is put up in *hogs' bladders*, and we buy a skin at a time. It is very sweet, and this method of procuring it is very good. If we could only know that the skins had been thoroughly cleaned!

VIII

VALPARAISO—VARIOUS INGREDIENTS

DECEMBER. We are comfortably settled in our new house on Cape Horn Hill, which is a great improvement on the old locality. We are two hundred feet above the sea, and look (twenty feet from our front door) down an abrupt hill bristling with cactuses, upon the housetops of the streets below. On either hand, the whole city lies in view; across a deep ravine are the Pantheons or burial grounds, while before stretches the bay with its shipping—and we see every vessel that goes out or comes in.

The mornings here are glorious, and the sunsets gorgeous. As most persons breakfast late, it is the custom to walk in the early morning before the wind rises. The hill promenades are then thronged with people inhaling the healthful breeze. Nowhere in the world, I think, can it be more charming than here upon these hills in the summer mornings, far above the vileness, dust, and tumult of the city. It is luxury to merely live and breathe in this golden sunshine viewing this magnificent scenery, and forgetting the troubles and struggles of the world beneath us.

From December until April the south wind blows. It usually rises about ten in the morning, and falls about five in the afternoon; but it often continues night and day for two or three days at a time—a furious wind, roaring about the house, penetrating every crevice, whirling the gravel and dust in clouds, and driving the red sand of the hills all over the bay and shipping. This south wind is remarkable for extending only about twenty-five miles inland, and one hundred and fifty miles seaward, and ranging along the coast from Cape Horn to the equator.

As it is now the summer of the south temperate zone, we are having the luxuries of June and July in December. Strawberries are brought to our door every day, and are

37

sold at a real (twelve and a half cents) a hundred—though the first that came were one dollar. The berry is very large, pale red in color, and firm in flesh, but it is deficient in flavor. Fruit is always sold by the number (even to strawberries) instead of by the measure; and at the close of all bargains it is the custom of the country (costumbre del país), for the seller to throw in a little extra of his commodity, for what they call the llapa. Chickens are brought to town tied together by the legs in bunches, like onions, slung upon the vendor's shoulder, and peddled from door to door, the merchant pinching their breasts with his nails to assure you of their flesh and tenderness. Turkeys are driven though the streets in large droves.

There is a very good Italian opera troupe now in Valparaiso, and we went the other evening to hear "Ernani." The theater is very handsome, and inside is not architecturally different from our own. Between the acts of the play or opera, the gentlemen go out into the vestibule, or upon the side, to indulge in the universal cigar, and a bell is rung to recall them before the curtain rises. The house is so filled with smoke for a few minutes after each act, that you can scarcely see across it. At the close of the performances all the gentlemen who have no ladies in charge, hurry into the vestibule, and take up their positions in a row, leaving a lane through which the ladies must pass, and stare at them with great earnestness, commenting often on their beauty. So far from considering this an impertinence, the Valparaiso fair think it very complimentary. Sundays and Thursdays are opera nights—Sunday night being the favorite with the Chilenos, when the best pieces are usually given. Theatergoing is an expensive amusement in Valparaiso. The price of a box is ten dollars, and you pay besides an *entrada* of one dollar and a quarter for each person.

JANUARY. It is now the 15th of the month, and mid-summer, and yet the mercury has not risen above 77° Fahrenheit. I paid a visit this morning to a lady who has a small yard filled with the choicest flowers, and brought home a magnificent bouquet of nineteen varieties—some of them familiar, and others I had never seen. She had heliotropes and fuschias five and six feet in height; and straw-colored tea roses covering a wall ten feet high, and blooming in clusters of four or five, each rose the size of a coffee saucer.

Peaches are now in season. All of them that I have seen are large but tasteless clingstones. All fruits and vegetables are brought from the Quillata Valley (some forty miles distant), on the backs of mules and donkeys, in panniers made of hide. A very fine, tall clover, called alfalfa, is cut and brought into the city to feed horses with. This, too, is carried on the backs of mules, in such quantities that nothing is to be seen of the animals but their feet and muzzled noses. The mule is used for every thing.

FEBRUARY. We have now very good pears, several kinds of plums, nectarines, melons, and grapes. The large, white grape of commerce is grown here in great perfection, as well as a fine purple grape, of which the clusters are prodigious in size. We have apples, but they are hard and sweet—good for nothing.

On the morning of the 4th of this month, we were aroused from sleep by a loud roar, and a jarring of the earth. In an instant we were on our feet, when there came another shock, yet more severe, rattling every door and window. The sensations produced by earthquakes are indescribable. In all other dangers, by sea and land, one has an instinctive feeling, that if it were only possible to touch mother earth, one would be safe, but when the earth herself quivers under our feet, the last refuge seems gone; all our preconceived notions of stability are shaken —we feel our utter helplessness; and to me the first idea was always of some crushing, overwhelming calamity— with a terror such as one might reasonably be expected to feel at the approach of the Day of Judgment.

I allow myself the greatest latitude of performance in these sketches of my life in Valparaiso, and I hope nobody will be astonished by my abrupt transitions from one subject to another. Our existence itself was as sudden in its passage from the sublime to the ridiculous, and back again —and now we were charmed with the delicious climate, and now disgusted with the dirty lanes and unwholesome people; now we shuddered at the throes of an earthquake, and now we bargained for poultry at the gate; now we mused among the groves of the pantheons, and now we strolled through the city diverted with its abounding and novel life.

One of the things which amused us in street sights, this month, was the variety of dress among the ladies. It was the autumn of the south temperate zone, but there was little change from the summer weather, and people dressed, some according to comfort, and some according to the season. One lady went by in a velvet dress, fur cloak and velvet hat—the full winter costume for a cold climate; another followed in a gay cashmere, and perhaps the next wore a lace bonnet and berage dress. The only thing in which they were all alike, was the long, voluminous skirts with which they swept the pavement far and wide.

Happily there is no such comment on the caprices of fashion in Valparaiso, as enlivens our newspaper literature at home—possibly because there are hardly any newspapers; there are only two Spanish dailies in the city, and all attempts to sustain a journal in English have failed.

IX

Holy Week and a "Norther"

April. The 9th of this month was Palm Sunday, and the week that followed was Holy Week, of great observance in all Catholic countries. All day Saturday the streets were filled with boys selling leaves of the coco palm, each about ten feet long, and braided and decorated with ribbons. On Sunday morning we went to the church of Nuestra Señora del Carmen, which we found thronged with kneeling figures of men and women, each bearing a leaf of palm, while dense masses of those who could not enter, blocked the doors. There were prayers intoned by the priests, music of polkas and waltzes, and abundance of waving of palms, but there was no sign of devotion, and no evidence that the people had in mind that day of which they were celebrating the anniversary. After awhile a priest entered the church, preceded by three dirty, bareheaded urchins, one of whom tinkled a little bell for the congregation to kneel, which they did as the procession passed them. Presently a band of music from the barracks arrived, when the crowd formed into a procession with the priests at their head, bearing a great book, and a palm gilt and crowned, and followed by boys with lighted tapers. Marching through the streets, they were joined by a procession from the church of La Merced; then after marching around the Plaza Victoria, they returned to the church, and the ceremonies for that day were concluded.

On Thursday morning, at ten o'clock, all places of business were closed; not a vehicle (unless that of a physician) was to be seen in the street, and all the Catholic ships in the harbor displayed their flags at half-mast. This was the anniversary of the crucifixion, and a solemn and sacred festival with the Catholic natives. Protestant foreigners usually spend it in picnic excursions, etc.

At night the churches were brilliantly illuminated; some parts of the ceremonies were very impressive. In front of the altar of the church we attended—the shrine blazing with candles—lay bound upon a cross, a life-size figure of the Saviour, carved in wood, and painted with all the horrors of His painful death. On either side of the image a guard was stationed, who cried at intervals, "Es tercera hora!" (It is the third hour.) People came and went in throngs, kissing the feet of the image.

It was a moonlight night; the streets were filled with multitudes, all mournfully attired in black, and groups of people repeated their prayers aloud, going from church to church—for the greater the number of these estaciones, as these visits are called, the greater the expiation.

On Friday the reign of silence continued, and the altars of the churches were draped in black. At night there was a torchlight procession. First came priests chanting, and then life-size images of the saints, clothed in flowing robes of velvet; among the rest was an image of the Virgin in white tarlatan, upon a platform, attended by four little girls, dressed as angels, with artificial wings, curls and flower wreaths upon their heads. The Holy Sepulchre was represented by a large box draped with white muslin, half revealing a recumbent figure. All these things were borne upon men's shoulders, and were succeeded by devotees with lanterns and candles, and surrounded by an unwholesome rabble, running and pushing, and jostling on every side.

On Saturday morning there were services in the churches, all gloomily decorated with black. The priests marched in procession—there was a vast deal of lighting and extinguishing of candles, tinkling of bells, genuflexions and swinging of censors, until ten o'clock, when suddenly the black veils before the altars were thrown aside, displaying the shrines all ablaze with candles, while the glad cry arose, "Christ is risen," and a peal of triumphant music burst from choir, organ, and bells. The cannon of the fort thundered the tidings, and the national ships of war re-echoed. The closed doors flew open, vehicles thronged the streets, business was resumed with its accustomed noise—

> And all the long-pent stream of life
> Dashed downward in a cataract,

while the indignant populace vented a retrospective rage upon effigies of Judas Iscariot, which were made to suffer every punishment that human ingenuity could invent —they were drowned in the sea, burnt at the corners, dragged through the streets, and torn to pieces on the hillsides.

And so ended Holy Week.

MAY. On Friday, the 7th, a "norther" commenced blowing, which, increasing through the night, on Saturday morning was most terrific. The bay opening to the north receives the full force of the wind—the waves roll upon the beach in the center, and hurl themselves upon the rocks at the extremities of the city, with a force that is seemingly irresistible. The water is very deep, and if vessels are not securely anchored, they are inevitably dashed to pieces upon the shore. There were some eighty ships and steamers in the bay, all rolling and plunging fearfully, with sheets of spray flying over their masts. Early in the morning, an old ship loaded with coals sunk at her moorings; and soon after another old vessel pulled her bows out and sunk. Later in the day, we observed a large ship gradually drawing near the breakers: ten minutes after she reached the first line, she was tossing in the furious surf of the beach like a cork, while her crew were plainly seen clinging to the masts and rigging. Hundreds of people thronged to the shore to render aid, and succeeded in stretching a rope from a mast to the beach, and by this means saved the crew. In two hours not a vestige of the vessel was to be seen; and before night three other ships were wrecked—so close in sight of us that we looked down upon their decks.

Many vessels were injured by collisions; and the rain

poured all day in torrents. At night the storm abated, and next morning the nearest mountain range was glittering with snow. After such a storm, the weather for several days is glorious—the snowy mountains glisten all day in the sun, and when the sun sets in the evening, they glow with all the hues and splendors of the rainbow—to fade slowly away, as night comes, into ghastly whiteness.

X

HOLIDAY HAPPENINGS

JUNE. The 29th of this month was St. Peter's Day, and was celebrated here with appropriate ceremonies. An image of St. Peter was placed in a boat gaily decorated with flags, and bearing several priests, which made the circuit of the bay, followed by a hundred other boats, likewise trimmed with banners. The image was plunged into the water and withdrawn, fumigated with incense, and taken back to the church. The figure was gigantic, and bore two immense keys in its hand. The object of this ceremony is, to bless the fish that they may increase and multiply.

Some of the Catholics here have a custom of expiating their sins by nine days' penance during Lent. In every town there is a house provided for the purpose, and in the charge of priests, where the penitents spend their nights in alternately praying and scourging each other. The infirm expiate their sins by reciprocal pinchings. The lights are extinguished, and at a signal from the priests the penitents change places and commence thrashing the nearest sinner with a vigor which cannot leave any doubt of the sincerity of their contrition. The devout often take a vow that if the Virgin will do certain things for them—restore a sick friend to health, or the like—they will perform this or that ceremony, or dress themselves or their children a specified length of time in a particular color. For instance, the French consul's wife having lost several children, vowed that if her last child was spared, she would clothe it in white for one year. It lived, and the vow was religiously fulfilled.

Many other pious observances attract the foreigner's attention. An American residing in an interior town, related that he saw a woman crawl on her naked knees round

45

an entire square—till her limbs streamed with blood—in penance for her sins.

SEPTEMBER. The 17th, 18th, and 19th of this month are required by government to be observed as national holidays. They are the anniversaries of the days when Chile threw off the Spanish yoke, and are celebrated with great rejoicings—the country people often continuing the holidays until October. Every house with pretensions to consideration has its flagstaff and banner waving over the street. The Chilean flag with its white star on blue ground, and one red and one white stripe, is very pretty; and the vast number of these, with the colors of the foreign officials, displayed during the festivities, give the city a beautiful appearance.

At this time, every woman must have a new dress, and every man a new poncho; houses are new painted, streets are cleaned, and the whole place furbished up, inside and out. Even our cook felt the contagion of reform, and I found her industriously pushing the dirt from the middle of the kitchen floor into the corners.

"What are you doing that for, María?" I asked.

"For the *diez y ocho*, señorita," was the reply.

On the 18th, the fort and all the men-of-war in the harbor fired a salute at sunrise; and at six, the National Anthem was sung in one of the plazas, by a hundred little girls in white. We spent that day at the house of a friend in the country, returning in time for the ceremonies of the 19th. Early in the morning of this last of the "diez y ocho," the whole population of Valparaiso thronged in holiday attire to the Plaza Ancha (broad plaza), where a grand military review was held. It was a beautiful spectacle, presented in full view of the great Pacific—thousands of military marching and countermarching, with music and streaming flags and flashing arms—men and women on horseback and in birlochos, and a joyous rout on foot, hurrying hither and thither with the restlessness of crowds, and entering and emerging from the innumerable gay refreshment booths that dotted the plaza.

This is the great day for the country people, when they display their horsemanship, and dance the Zama-cueca, the national dance of Chile. Pausing in front of one of the booths, we went in and found a man and woman from the country engaged in the dance—he with spurs and poncho, and she in a Panama hat, gaily trimmed with ribbons, and her long riding skirt thrown over her arm. Two women were making the music for them—one upon a rude harp, and the other upon a guitar, accompanying the instruments with strong, nasal voices, while a man beat time with his palms upon a board. It is difficult to describe the dance, which consists of a succession of advancing and receding steps, the dancers alternately pursuing each other, and occasionally twirling a handkerchief in the right hand.

The country people are very skilful riders, and there is no feat of horsemanship which they cannot perform. When they are a little excited with *chicha*, it is dangerous to be in their way. The men sometimes run their horses at full speed upon a mounted gentleman, and as they pass him, catch a knee inside of his, and unless he is on his guard, unhorse him in an instant, to their immense delight. It is a common thing to see women, on holidays, racing together on horseback. They all bring their horses into line, and then applying the whip, set off at a furious gallop.

OCTOBER. We attended a great national ball at the theater on the 1st, to which tickets, admitting a gentleman and his family, were sold at one ounce ($17.25), the courtesy of purchase being extended only to guests selected by the committee. The pit of the theater was floored and carpeted, and the first tier of boxes, screened with velvet hangings, served as dressing rooms, while flags of all nations gracefully draped from the upper gallery. Two fine bands of music were stationed at either end of the room. At ten o'clock, when we arrived, only few persons were present, but at eleven the dancing commenced. The appearance of the guests (many of whom were from Santiago) was most brilliant. The ladies were all robed in gauzes, laces, and silks, made in the latest Parisian mode, and blazing with diamonds. I thought the most tasteful dress in the room was a flounced white lace wrought in gold, and worn over white silk, with golden heads of wheat in the dark hair of the wearer. Officials, native and foreign, in their rich uniforms, contributed to the splendor of the scene.

Waltzes, gallopades, mazurkas, and quadrilles were the dances—the quadrille, with the ends and sides sometimes doubled and trebled. At twelve o'clock a room for the refreshments of tea and cakes was thrown open, and at two a magnificent supper was set, consisting of every delicacy to be obtained in the country. At four in the morning, we retired among the first—several urging us to remain for another *supper*. On the first floor, tables were spread with cold meats and liquors, which were kept replenished for gentlemen all night.

DECEMBER. On Christmas we attended midnight mass at the church of La Matriz. Arraying ourselves in black, with black shawls drawn over our heads, we entered the brilliantly lighted church, which we found densely crowded with kneeling men and women. Struggling with the worshippers to the center of the church, we stood there until exhausted, when an old woman kindly shared her mat with us. The ceremonies continued for two hours— consisting of a sermon and the peculiar forms of the church. (*En passant*—all Chileno crowds, religious and secular, are distinguished by two things: an overpowering stench of garlic, and the presence of innumerable fleas.) Outside of the church, during the ceremony, boys and men were blowing horns and springing rattles, and making every other hideous noise imaginable.

MAY. On the 27th, a murderer was shot in the Plaza del Orden, which lies at the foot of our hill. Thousands assembled on the hillsides, housetops, and every available spot to witness the execution. The criminal, clothed in a long white robe, and accompanied by three holy fathers, was led to a post, seated with his back against it, and his body and arms tied to it. Eight soldiers were drawn up in front, and at a signal, four of them fired at his heart—a drooping of his head was the only preceptible motion that followed the discharge. I had no intention of witnessing so horrible a spectacle, but looking with a glass to see how the man was secured, the soldiers fired before I could withdraw my eyes. This is the mode of execution in Chile.

XI

To Santiago and Return

On the 4th of September, 1855, we left Valparaiso for a brief visit to Santiago, the Chilean capital, where we proposed to spend the "diez y ocho." Until within a year, birlochos had been the only means of conveyance for persons going to the capital, but now the journey was made by a regular daily line of coaches, established by an American, and furnished with Yankee stages and Yankee drivers. The departure of the coach was always a great event at Valparaiso—a crowd of ever-astonished Chilenos assembling every day to witness the phenomenon of one man driving six horses.

The transportation of merchandise and other freight from Valparaiso to Santiago is effected by means of enormous oxcarts, bamboo-bodied, and roofed with hide. They are usually drawn by three yoke—the leading yoke to be detached and hitched to the tail of the cart as a "holdback" in descending the hills.

We quitted Valparaiso at noon, having quite a cosmopolitan company of passengers—three Peruvians, two Italians, one half-Chileno, and four Americans. Passing out at the east of the city, we ascended the rising road until we had reached an elevation of thirteen hundred feet, whence we looked back upon the dusty city beneath us, and the bay flashing in the sun and flecked with far, white sails, while upon the right, the snow-crested Aconcagua lifted its stately peak, about which hovered a blush of faint, delicious crimson.

The face of these hills is barren—but for now and then a nook of green where a tall, solitary palm lifts its graceful head above a little stream, and with here and there a wide-armed, stone windmill, gives to the desolate landscape its only element of the picturesque.

After a descent of some five miles, we arrived at a little posada, or country inn, where we exchanged our six tired horses for four fresh ones, and continued our journey. The recent rains had made fresh and green the fields that, two months hence, would be parched and brown with heat; and now the south wind blew so strong and cool that we were obliged to close the coach windows.

At six o'clock we reached Casablanca, thirty miles from Valparaiso. The posada here is kept by an English couple, to whom we were introduced by a fellow passenger. They received us with cordiality, and took us into their own part of the inn, where we fared better than if left to the mercies of the servants in the travelers' rooms. The posada is a one-story house, comfortable, pleasantly furnished, and with actually a carpet on the parlor floor. As the night was cool, a large brasero was kept burning in our room, and we had a good English supper of beef steak, eggs, toast, and tea. The eating, I say, was English —the sleeping was decidedly Chileno, in a forlorn brick-floored, dirtily carpeted room, upon hard, narrow beds, which I ache to remember.

Casablanca is situated upon an elevated plain, and contains about two thousand inhabitants. The road to Santiago (which forms the principal street) is lined on either side with Lombardy poplars for miles.

We were on the road again at four o'clock next morning, and traveled until daylight over a level country, which then began to grow more rolling. The road, the hillsides and plains, in some places, are covered with shrubs, giant cactuses, and espino trees, which resemble old apple trees. The road was thronged with oxcarts, and men and women on horseback—the women riding the native saddle, which has a back and no horns, and sitting on the wrong side, their bodies at right angles with the horses' head. Among other wayfarers were chicken merchants, driving mules, each laden with a large coop. These poulterers, in traveling, stop on the plains near a stream, let their chickens out, feed them, drive them to water—and have all the life of the barnyard about them. Then restoring the fowls to their coops, they set off again.

At eleven o'clock we reached Melipilla, a town of one-story adobe houses, whitewashed and tile-roofed. It contains nearly eight thousand inhabitants, and is a place of considerable wealth. Here we had a miserable breakfast of cazuela and coffee. Cazuela is a national dish, used everywhere in Chile, and is a sort of stew made of chicken commonly (though sometimes of other meats), with potatoes, rice, and green peas.

From Melipilla to Santiago is an almost imperceptible ascent. The sides of the road are lined with ditches of running water, and bordered by long rows of poplars and mud walls. The walls are made of mud taken from the ditch, packed in a frame, and turned out until the wall is of sufficient height; they are then sometimes roofed with tile, and make excellent fencing, in a climate where there is no frost to crack them. Other fences are made of stakes interlaced with espino bushes.

The poplar trees grow readily from cuttings, and are planted so thickly that, when they are of full size, they are not more than two feet apart. Occasionally we saw a rancho or farmhouse by the road side, built of adobes, or of sticks and mud, and thatched with straw. Stopping at one of them to change horses, we entered. The ground served for a floor; there was a rude bedstead in one corner of the room, and three or four chairs; a fire of charcoal was burning on the ground, and over it stood a long-legged iron pot, and near this a couple of round, reddish earthen jars, the sole cooking utensils. Two or three women were standing about, with apparently nothing to do. They were polite and hospitable—asking if we were going to Santiago to spend the "diez y ocho," wishing us enjoyment, and presenting us with oranges. Near the hut, a few apple, pear and peach trees were in bloom.

We saw a few countryseats—large, low houses, surrounded with fruit trees. These places are the residences of the hacendados, or landed proprietors, and all have

distinguished names, such as San Pedro, San Isidro, etc.
For miles along the road on either hand stretched boundless fields of clover, in which thousands of cattle were feeding.

At four in the afternoon, passing through the low suburbs of Santiago, we drove up in front of a pair of wide
iron gates—the entrance to the Hotel Inglés—a large
building in the Plaza de la Independencia; here we found
our rooms (engaged three weeks before) very comfortable.
They opened upon an inner patio and the corridor, from
which latter the giant crests of the Andes were visible.
That evening we feasted our vision upon a scene of sub-
limity and beauty that alone repaid us a thousandfold
for all we had endured in coming to Chile. The sun was
sinking in the west, and flashing his last crimson rays
upon those majestic peaks, whose snows gleamed and
sparkled in the tender light, as the broad white wings of
hovering angels might shine, in the descent from heaven.
But even as we looked, the glories of the scene passed
away, the sun sank beneath the horizon, and the mountains rose, pale and phantomlike, in the deepening twilight.

Santiago, seven miles square, lies on a plain at the
foot of the Andes—several spurs of which are inclosed
within the city limits. Santa Lucia, a pyramidal hill of
rock, rises one hundred and eighty feet above the plaza.
It is crowned with a mass of prismatic porphyry, inclining at an angle of forty-five degrees, looking as if the first
temblor would precipitate it upon the houses below. This
hill is the site of the observatory established by Lieutenant
Gilliss, on the part of our government, for the purpose of
taking astronomical observations. On the sides of the hill
are forts now disused.

The river Mapocho divides the city. In the dry season there is a small quantity of water flowing through
many channels; during the winter, the rains raise the river
to a rapid and angry flood. High breakwaters are built
on either side of the stream to prevent inundations, which

have destroyed a large part of the city. The river is spanned by a massive stone bridge of eleven arches, built in the year 1775, which is 650 feet long, and wide enough for footways, and the passage of two carts abreast. The road-way is paved with stone, and upon each abutment on the stream are little brick towers, originally intended as guard-houses, to protect the bridge against Indians, but are now used as shops, where edibles of all descriptions are sold.

The streets of Santiago are comparatively wide, and are paved with round stones. They were lighted with oil when we were there, but gas was soon to be introduced. The buildings are mostly of adobe, and roofed with tile—seldom exceeding one story in height—a circumstance that of course conduces to safety in earthquakes. Building stone is abundant, but the mechanics are not skilful in working it. The houses of the wealthy are constructed in the Span-ish fashion, with patios inclosed by the different apart-ments of the house, and usually filled with flowering shrubs, having a magnolia or some other fine tree in the center. The entrance is by means of large iron gates, broad and high enough to admit a mail coach, which are left open by day, and closed at night. In several of the houses we visited, the stable was on one side of the gates, and the porter's room on the other. Passing through the patio we entered the parlors, beyond which was another patio, filled with plants, and accessible from the dining room and bedchambers—and those with the servants' rooms and kitchens sometimes inclosed a third patio. In the first, just before the parlor windows, the carriage was cleaned and the horses harnessed. The patios are paved with round pebbles from the Mapocho, and have in the center some-times a fanciful figure, or a date, formed of the extremities of the leg bones of mules. The houses are very unpretend-ing in appearance outside, as the building material does not admit of much architectural display. Square tiles laid upon the ground are universally used for flooring, while the ceilings are always of board, for plastering would be shaken off by earthquakes. The walls are plastered with mud, and then every apartment is papered. Within doors, every luxury that wealth can procure, the rich have. Furniture is brought from France;—one Chileno of whom I heard furnished two parlors with Parisian furniture, at an expense of thirty-four thousand dollars.

Some of the public buildings of Santiago are very fine. A new theater, building while we were there, was to be the largest in the world. A penitentiary, recently finished, is two miles from the city. It is built of brick, in octagon form, inclosing a court which serves for a chapel. There are cells for five hundred and thirty prisoners. Of course, the building is only one story in height. The mint, built in Doric style, is the most imposing public edifice. In this the President of Chile resides. A noticeable building is the Portal, on one of the plazas—an immense affair, in which most of the splendid shops are to be found, and where every thing that can be imported is for sale.

There are many churches, but none of them remarkable for beauty. The Cathedral is an imposing edifice, of gray granite, fronting on the principal plaza. Although one hundred years old, it is not yet finished, and workmen were still engaged upon it when we were there. Two rows of columns support the roof, within. There are sixteen altars in the side aisles, and one lofty shrine in the center of the building, which is richly decorated with massive silver candlesticks, silver vases, silver frames on which to rest the books of prayer—and over all, resting upon a heavy silver cornice, a canopy of the same precious metal. Under one of the aisles lie buried three bishops, whose enormous shovel hats, begrimed with dust are suspended from the roof above the sepulchres.

As we sauntered through the building, we were accosted by a young man apparently in office there, who asked us if we would like to see a relic; we were anxious, of course, and a curtain was drawn aside from a little recess, where we beheld a recumbent skeleton, of small size, brown with age, and decorated with gauze, tinsel, and faded flowers. This, we were assured, was Saint Mark.

There are extant several skeletons of this Evangelist, but we were very glad to see *one*. Upon a table in front of every church in Santiago stands a figure of the Virgin, with a little box for alms. The interiors of the churches are ornamented with figures of saints, the Virgin, and the Saviour —the latter often depicted in agonies of death upon the cross.

In a chapel adjoining the Cathedral, we were shown a splendid painting of Pope Pius IX, which was ordered in Italy for Louis Phillippe, but was not finished before his flight from France, when it was purchased by a gentleman and presented to this Cathedral. There are said to be three thousand priests in Santiago.

One morning, an American gentleman, who has long been a resident of the place, came for us with his carriage, and took us three miles into the country, to his quinta, or countryseat. The mansion was one story, large in dimensions, and square in shape, with large rooms plainly furnished. A corridor ran along the western side of the house. The kitchen was a hut, about forty feet from the dining room door. A broad avenue of poplars led from the road to the house, through massive gates, near which stood a thatched porter's lodge, with squalid children lying about in the sun.

The first industrial exhibition was held during our stay in Santiago. The show was very poor—consisting for the most part of a few flowers, specimens of embroidery, and poor paintings. A noticeable feature was a figure of the Saviour, of life-size, habited in flowing robes, and wearing under the crown of thorns, long curls of brown ribbons.

The sewerage of the city consists of ditches in the middle of alternate streets, in which the garbage from the houses is thrown; at eight o'clock every evening water is let into the ditches from gates in the Tajomar above the city, which rushes rapidly along, and carries all the filth into the river below. At right angles with these ditches are others passing under the rows of houses between the guttered streets. Although this system of sewerage is good, the carelessness of officials often permits the drains to become clogged, and the stench becomes intolerable.

The city has command of an unlimited supply of water, but the earthen pipes that convey it are constantly out of order, and the water is turbid. The rich have filters made of a kind of porous stone abounding on the coast north of Coquimbo. Dripping through these filters into earthen jars, the water in this dry climate becomes so cool that no ice is necessary. For purposes of luxury, snow mixed with hail is brought into the city daily from the Andes, a distance of four leagues, on mules which carry fifty pounds each, inclosed in straw between frames of hide network. It is used for making ices—of which the favorite is water ice, flavored with coffee or chocolate.

Fronting the Cañada is the Hospital of San Juan de Dios, with accommodations for six hundred patients. It is spaciously and comfortably arranged, but the rooms are badly ventilated. San Francisco de Borja is a hospital for women, with accommodations for five hundred. It is not so well contrived in any respect as the other. There is a foundling hospital in Santiago, where infants are left day and night, without any possibility of detection from within, by means of a revolving box, in a wall, and a tap to call the attention of the porter; the box is turned within, and the babe is received, never more to be recognized by the one who leaves it. Almost five hundred children are thus annually abandoned by their parents in Santiago. "As the convents," says Lieut. Gilliss, in his interesting work on Chile, "are barred to all persons of the male sex (and indeed to the female also), except the Archbishop, the Doctor, and to the new President, for a single visit, I took occasion to examine the arrangements of their intended domicile before they moved into it. The apartments open on long corridors, which communicate with extensive chambers for the use of the Abbess, and in bad weather afford them places for exercise. Each nun has a small sitting-room, a dormitory, and a servants' room, with conveniences for cooking, washing, and stowage of household necessities, a stream of water passing through the premises of every one.

"The luxuriously disposed keep a servant, who is free to return to the world when tired of cloistral labor, but is not at liberty to go back and forth each day.

"For the supply of their necessities, a sort of market is held daily, in a court of their property specially provided, and hither are brought for sale, provisions and materials, and such articles as their industry embraces. Neither purchaser nor seller sees the other, but the commodity offered is placed within one of the recesses of a turnstile, filling an aperture of the wall, and if accepted, its value is returned in the same manner.

"Many of the nuns are skilled in needlework, and in making ornamental pastilles, fancy toys of earthenware, and confectionery of various kinds, in the sale of which they employ servants outside.

"In 1850, the convent numbered 75 nuns, and 176 seculars."

I was told that in one convent of the Capuchins, applicants are only received upon the payment of two thousand five hundred dollars. They sleep in holes made in the earth of the size of their bodies, with a cloth around them, and a stone for a pillow. If they encounter, when walking in their yard, their salutation is: "We are to die," and "We know it." Many of them die early from the hardships of such a life, and their money goes to the institution.

There are seven monasteries and eight convents in Santiago, wherein five hundred women are shut out from the world.

The cemetery is a mile and a half from the plaza. About fifteen acres of ground, inclosed by high walls, are divided into lots by iron railings, for monuments, families, and the poor. In the cemetery are a chapel and buildings for workmen, a pretty garden, and rows of cypress trees. There are a few handsome mausoleums of marble, one of which is surmounted by a nude figure of Grief, executed in white marble. By an order of the Archbishop, this statue has been covered with a petticoat of white cloth, from the waist to the knees. As at Valparaiso, there are perpetual sepulchres, graves for one year, and for the poor the bone pit.

In regard to education in Santiago, I quote Lieut. Gilliss, who says:

"The National Institute numbers 900 pupils, of whom 260 are internos, and live wholly within its walls. The remainder are day scholars. To conduct the establishment there is a rector, a vice-rector, and thirty-six professors, all receiving their appointment and pay from government.

"Instruction is free to all—the internos only being subject to $150 per annum for their board. Corporal punishment is not permitted. Among the gravest offenses specified are, not retiring at the appointed hour, leaving the Institute without permission, and neglect to confess at the appointed times; among the lightest are uncleanliness, and disrespect to their companions. Latin, Greek, English, French, arithmetic, algebra, trigonometry, geography, cosmography, drawing, history, rhetoric, and moral philosophy; religion, music, and the elements of physics, chemistry, mineralogy, and natural history are taught.

"The course occupies six years. Connected with the Institute is a normal school under the direction of the Minister of Public Instruction; twenty-eight young men are prepared here as teachers for the provinces. The course occupies three years, vaccination being one of the subjects of instruction. There are a number of boarding and day schools, under the direction of convents and individuals, which are well patronized. Besides these, there are thirty-five primary institutions at the cost of the municipality. The last, as almost all the day schools for the humbler class, are held in rooms badly lighted, and worse ventilated, of whose vicinity one becomes aware at a long distance, by the loud voices of all the children conning their lessons at the same time."

There are, in the Republic of Chile, without count-
ing Araucanian Indians, 1,439,120 inhabitants, of whom
there are 13,256 more women than men. Of all the inhabitants of the Republic, 123,437 men, and 70,461 women,
can read; total, 193,898—leaving 1,245,222 individuals
of both sexes who cannot read.

An academy was established in 1842 for the education of officers destined to service in the army and navy.
Sixty cadets are educated at the expense of the State, but
supernumeraries are admitted, and the number of actual
students of the academy is twice that expressed in the
statutes. There are, besides, schools under government
patronage for instruction in the mechanic arts, agricul-
ture, painting, and music. The national library at the
capital contains about twenty-one thousand volumes,
which are accessible to the public from ten till one every
day. No one is permitted to remove a volume from the
building, though every facility is afforded for making ex-
tracts.

In the way of journals, there was, when we visited
Santiago, one newspaper, *El Araucano*, as large as one of
our smallest dailies. It is the official organ, and rarely pub-
lishes anything but laws and decrees, and the reports of
congressional proceedings. Two small monthly periodicals were devoted, one to the Catholic religion, and one to
musical and dramatic criticisms.

Very few foreigners, beside the diplomatic corps of
some four or five countries, reside in Santiago, and the
streets present an appearance very different from that of
the port of Valparaiso, where there is much of the bustle
and activity of one of our American cities. Early in the
morning the women, in their black dresses and montos—
a large black shawl worn over the head and shoulders (no
other color than black is ever worn to church)—throng
the streets on their way to mass, and hundreds of peones
from the country, noisily cry their wares. As noon approaches, the heat of the sun drives everybody within
doors, where the people remain until its declining rays

permit them to issue forth again. Night and day the clangor of church bells is incessant—as if it were a dogma of the mother church to make all the clashing possible, and to destroy the slumber of heretic foreigners.

All Spanish cities are much alike, whether in the old or new world—one of their invariable features is an avenue adorned with trees, for promenading. The Alameda, or Cañada of Santiago, is a broad walk about two miles in extent, with seats at intervals, under the triple lines of poplars on either side, of which the roots are bathed with streams of running water from the mountains. Streets five hundred feet in breadth, lie between the poplars and the houses. Hither in the twilight or the moonlight comes the fair Santiaguina to promenade and display her finery— often wearing in the summer a full ball costume. In these charming avenues, people meet their acquaintances, sit or walk, as they choose, and enjoy social intercourse in the pure air, with the glorious mountains in full view. A walk in the Cañada is the daily custom when the weather permits. On either side of the avenues, the *ton* dash up and down in their carriages, with coachmen and footmen in livery. Indeed, no family in Santiago can pretend to respectability without keeping a carriage, and many of the equipages, imported from France and England, are magnificent.

The 17th of October was ushered in by the firing of cannons from the forts on Santa Lucia, which simultaneously displayed the national flag, and soon the city was gay with the banners that fluttered from every housetop. This patriotism is in part compulsory, for there is a fine of from one to twenty dollars for failure to show a flag. Foreign ministers raise the colors of their respective governments, but resident foreigners, undistinguished by official rank, are allowed to flaunt none but the Chileno standard.

On the 18th, at sunrise, the national air was sung by one hundred little boys and girls, in the Plaza de la Independencia. At noon there was a grand *misa de gracia* in the

Cathedral. All the foreign diplomats (many of them in superb military dress) were present. The President arrived in his coach-and-four, escorted by a battalion of soldiers, and a detachment of cadets from the national military academy, who formed his bodyguard. Entering the church, he seated himself in a large chair covered with crimson and gold, in the main aisle, fronting the central altar—two of the cadets, with fixed bayonets, taking position on either side. His Excellency was dressed in plain black frock coat and trousers, with a tricolor scarf passing over his shoulder, and having a chapeau plumed with one white ostrich feather. As part of the ceremony, the President was presented with a book and cross to kiss; the osculation being repeated by each of the officials, while at the same time they were all fumigated with incense.

The ceremonies occupied two hours, and the evening closed with illuminations, and a grand display of fireworks on the plaza.

On the 20th, the President reviewed the troops—the plain Pampilla, two miles from Santiago, being used annually for military reviews, which are always a great spectacle to the thousands, who flock to witness them from country and city. As we passed through the streets on our way to the Pampilla, every thing wore a holiday aspect. Gay crowds thronged the way, and the pulperías and confectionery shops swarmed with customers. Meanwhile, the guasos and guasitos, or country lads and lasses, galloped from their homes to the parade ground on horseback, and country families soberly followed in their primitive carriages—a kind of cart, of which the body and roof are made of boards, or bamboo and hide, with windows in the side, and curtains shielding the openings in front and rear—while the interior is made comfortable with hides. This vehicle is drawn by a yoke of oxen, whose driver, with his conical straw hat, poncho, and goad fifteen feet long, is a *cosa de ver*. Sometimes notes of the guitar, accompanied, with very bad singing, proceeded from these carriages.

On the grounds we found some six or seven thousand

military drawn up in front of two lines of oxcarts, at least a mile in extent, with sufficient room between them for promenading and riding. Awnings were stretched from cart to cart, forming booths, where cakes, fruit, and chicha were sold, harps twangled, and the cueca danced, while mounted peddlers, with panniers of every conceivable commodity—guasos dashing about at fearful speed—*beggars on horseback*—and carriages filled with joyous people, contributed to form a scene of rare confusion and gaiety.

At two o'clock, the President and his staff arrived; the review took place, and the troops, after a grand *feu de joie*, marched back to the city, followed by an immense crowd, while thousands of the country people remained on the Pampilla, for a week of frolic and carousal.

In the evening, we walked in the Alameda, which was thronged with six or seven thousand promenaders, while elegant dresses, with the brilliant uniforms of the naval and army officers, and the state dresses of the foreign diplomats, made the beautiful avenue gayer than ever.

Santiago is immensely rich—richer perhaps, according to its population of 130,000, than any other city on this continent. The Chileno has few inducements to travel in his own country, and little ambition to go abroad. The great object of life is to accumulate wealth, and remove to the capital, to lavish it in costly furniture, equipage, and splendid living.

As Santiago is more elevated than Valparaiso, it is subject to greater extremes of heat and cold; and during the hot months of December, January, and February, the rich retire to their quintas, or to Valparaiso for the sea bathing.

Manuel Montt, the President of the Republic during our stay in Chile, was then nearly sixty years of age. He was the first civilian who had filled the presidential chair, and was a gentleman of fine ability and liberal views.

On the 24th of October, we bade adieu to Santiago, and returned to Valparaiso by a different route from that we had traveled in coming. From Casablanca there are two roads to the capital—the stagecoach route, long but comparatively safe, and the other passing over the famous Cuesta del Prado, which is traveled usually in gigs, and is rather dangerous. We thought we would risk its perils for the sake of its novelties, and so determined to take the latter road. At first we intended to charter birlochos, but I dreaded the fatigue, and we finally took passage with a Frenchman, who drove a coach regularly between the cities. We hired his vehicle (which he called the Golondrina Chilena, or Chilean Swallow), and he pledged himself to drive just as we desired, and stop when we wished— which he of course utterly failed to do.

At nine o'clock in the morning, we started from the hotel with three horses abreast, and in the suburbs stopped while three more horses were attached to our vehicle—one on either side of the first three, and the third, bestridden by a peon in a scarlet poncho, made fast to the carriage tongue in front, with a thong of twisted hide some ten or twelve feet in length. We had then five horses abreast— no two of the same size or color, but all bruised and beaten till spotted—the harness a bewildering miscellany of leather and rope, inscrutably attached to the coach and horses—and all under the guidance of the mounted peon. Our Gaul, who was to take no passengers but ourselves, begged us to allow him to have two friends with him in front. We weakly consented, and away we went, through squalid streets of adobe huts, and avenues of poplar, until we reached an open plain, which on this side of the city is arid and uninteresting.

The road was broad and dusty, the whip was constantly applied, and with our horses on a swift gallop, their heels flying in the air on either side of our coach, and our driver shrieking "Fuego al campo!" (fire to the plain), we ascended gradually for twenty-one miles to the foot of the cuesta. Here a relay of horses were feeding on a little piece of pasturage, and our peon was detached to drive them to the summit, when we were to change teams. Now commenced the real ascent. The road is about forty feet

wide inclining to the hill, and we wound up and up, turn-
ing sharp corners and plunging through deep gorges,
whose green banks were gay with flowers, and bristling
with giant cactuses, till at last we reached the summit of
twenty-four hundred feet; and while our driver was chang-
ing horses, alighted to look back over the route we had
traveled. A verdant basin lay in an amphitheater of green
hills, with Santiago in the center; scarcely perceptible at
this great distance amid its dark green poplars, while far
beyond rose the mighty Andes, glittering between fleecy
clouds in the morning sun. The air was bright and pure
and sweet, and I felt that glorious exaltation of the spirit,
which the subtlest and deepest of our poor utterances cannot describe.

Regretfully we mounted again into our vehicle, and
resumed our journey. We had now in front three horses
abreast; and behind, two attached to the coach with
halters to retard our descent. The zigzags were short and
steep, and the angles so acute that, as we whirled furiously
around them, our wheels gave out a harsh, whizzing
sound that thrilled every nerve; but down we went, never
once pausing, on a rapid trot, our Frenchman, who was to
drive just as we wanted, declaring that he would beat the
locomotive. As we neared the level ground again, the zigzags grew longer; our horses were again hitched in front,
and we dashed away over the dusty road through a country of sparsely covered shrubs and stunted trees, with here
and there a squalid hut of mud and sticks, until twelve
o'clock, when we entered the town of Curacavi, twenty
miles from Santiago. In this cluster of adobe hovels, we
remained long enough to lunch and exchange for fresh
horses. After a travel of some miles further, the monotony
of which was only varied by meeting oxcarts, laden with
merchandise, we arrived at the foot of the Cuesta Zapata,
and while our *cochero* halted again for fresh horses, we
alighted to rest ourselves by walking. Following a path
made by the cattle, we ascended a part of the mountain,
while our coach followed the windings of the road. This

cuesta is eighteen hundred and fifty feet above the sea, and from the top, looking down the western side, the zigzags are all seen at once, resembling an immense stairway. Some fifty oxcarts were ascending and descending, in the distance looking like giant bees, crawling along the sides of a gigantic beehive. Encountering these carts is one of the perils of the road, but we descended this cuesta more slowly than the other, and although we came in collision with one of the carts, no damage was done. Reaching the plain, we crossed a stream of water, now insignificant, but which, with a few hours' rain, becomes an impassable torrent.

The ten miles to Casablanca we traveled at a gallop, never resting a moment—the whip going, the horses' heels flying in close proximity to our windows, and the scarlet poncho of our driver gallantly streaming in the wind. It was twilight when we drew up in front of the posada at Casablanca—very tired, but extremely thankful to have arrived in safety. On the following day, reached Valparaiso at noon.

XII

Features of Valparaiso

The great event of the foreigner's life at Valparaiso, is the semimonthly arrival of the mail steamer, bringing news from home. We long eagerly for the day she is expected, and hail with rapture the first breath of her smoke on the distant horizon. As she reaches her anchorage, we watch with a glass the transfer of the mailbags to the boat, and calculate the moments which must elapse before we receive our letters.

While we were in Santiago, the opening of the Valparaiso and Santiago Railroad (which had been completed as far as Viña del Mar), was celebrated with great pomp and religious ceremonies, the engines being blessed and sprinkled with holy water by the bishop himself. The road as surveyed is one hundred and twenty miles in length. It was commenced in 1852, and before we left Chile, had been finished to Quillota, a distance of forty miles, at a cost of $3,500,000. The estimated expense of completing the road to Santiago is $5,500,000. The engines were brought from England, and the passenger cars from Belgium. The latter were similar to our old stagecoaches, in shape and capacity, trimmed with fine drab cloth, and highly finished. The second class cars were merely bodies, furnished with seats and without roofs. The road for some distance runs at the foot of a rocky bluff, and is protected on the side next the sea by a massive wall of masonry; passing then through a short tunnel and a deep cut, the cars arrive at Viña del Mar, seven miles from Valparaiso. This has always been a favorite resort with pleasure seekers, who used to come hither on horseback, every Sunday and feast day. Since the road is completed, Viña del Mar has been more popular than ever; and one day we made an excursion to the place. It is a little valley upon an arm of the sea, watered by a small stream, and has several posadas, eating houses, and countryseats belonging to people of the city. One of these latter, the proprietress kindly gave us permission to visit. It was in the rainy season, and the valley was beautifully green, while the hillsides were gay with flowers. From the road we passed through a long avenue of poplars, entering a yard in front of a large, low adobe house, with a corridor in front. Behind the mansion was a small plat of ground, adorned with all the choice flowers of this and other countries, in full bloom. The flowers were in beds, with elevated, narrow paths between, and each surrounded with a little ditch for irrigation. Beyond this yet, on the hill slope, under the shade of some small trees, was built a bath of masonry, through which flowed a mountain rivulet, giving life and freshness to the gay parterre below. We procured some bread and cheese at one of the cafes, and with strawberries from a bed near us, we made our dinner in the shade of an immense fig tree that rose forty feet above us; and so returned to the city.

On the 16th, there was a grand procession at Valparaiso, in honor of the Immaculate Conception. All the images of the churches were borne through the streets on men's shoulders. One figure of the Virgin had a new dress for the occasion made of a flowing robe of blue silk, with curls of ribbon falling to her shoulders, a wreath of flowers on the head, and long ribbons passed around the waist, and terminating in the hands of two little girls representing angels in the act of leading the Virgin. A woman intended to represent Judith, carried a hideous counterfeit of Holofernes's head in one hand, and a large knife in the other. Many priests followed in their robes, chanting; and an immense rabble of the devout packed the narrow streets, and moved confusedly to different measures of music—the band performing "Bowery Girls," among other solemn pieces, with great distinctness.

XIII

Mining and Money

"The portion of Chile, north of the Valley of Huasco," says Lieutenant Gilliss, "is the richest in mineral wealth, particularly silver. In 1850, there were worked in the department of Copiapó, two hundred and ninety mines of silver, six of gold, and thirty of copper. Chañarcillo is considered the richest silver mine in the world. It was discovered in 1832, by a man hunting goats. He sat down to rest on a projecting rock that gave way, and disclosed the pure silver. This mine also yields mercury, copper, bismuth, tin, lead, arsenic, cobalt—in fact, almost the whole range of minerals are found within its depths.

"The province of Coquimbo is one of the most productive copper districts in the world, and with more skilful engineers and suitable machinery, the more precious metals could be obtained in a remunerative quantity.

"The region between the parallels of 30° and 31° south latitude, and 74° of longitude, is filled with veins of gold, silver, quicksilver, copper, and other rare combinations of metals. I shall only mention two—Arqueros and Algodones, one to the north and the other to the south of Coquimbo river. They were accidentally discovered by a hunter stumbling over some rolling stones containing a large percentage of silver, lying at the bottom of a ravine. When his good luck became known, a crowd went to the spot and picked up 10,000 dollars' worth of ore from the surface. Soon after the vein from which these stones came was discovered, and also two others, since which time they have yielded in all more than four millions of dollars. There are gold and salt mines to the south among the Araucanians, but the former are not worked. Iron is found in small quantities.

"Valuable coal mines exist half way between Talcahuano and Concepción, on the river Andalien; the coal is of good quality, and the position such that boats can be loaded from the mouth of the mine.

"Extensive coal deposits also exist at Coronel and Colcura, a few leagues south of the Bío-Bío, on the coast."

The coal is extremely inflammable, and the engineers complain that it burns out their fire bars. It is taken to Valparaiso, Santiago, and California in large quantities, and is delivered on board ship, at five dollars a ton.

In the northern provinces of Chile, there is almost unlimited wealth in silver and copper, but owing to the scarcity of water and fuel in many places, and the great difficulty of transporting the product, many of the mines have been abandoned, while others yield but a small profit. Nevertheless, speculation in mining sometimes almost amounts to mania; in many cases owners become discouraged—think they do not acquire wealth rapidly enough —and sell out at a low figure, and the purchaser perhaps strikes a rich lode, and doubles his investment. There are proprietors of mines living at Santiago, whose income is so enormous that they are ignorant of the exact amount.

Smelting, where there is fuel, is sometimes done at the mines, but usually at the port, and much metal is shipped in a crude state. Trains of mules laden with silver and copper ore in bags, or smelted bars, under military escort, and headed, each train, by an old mare, called the madrina—to whose neck a little bell is hung—wend their way through the mountains and over the rugged country, bearing their precious cargoes to the ports. On their return the mules are tied heads to tails and never losing the sound of the madrina's bell, slowly and patiently regain the mines. In Valparaiso the bar silver passes through the hands of the British consul, and I have seen upon the floor of his office a pile of silver bars fifteen feet long, four feet high, and four feet wide, each bar valued at from $2,200, to $2,500.

The currency of Chile is metallic. The silver is decimal like our own, and quite as handsome. Formerly there

were silver coins in circulation, which were made by drop-
ping melted silver on a hard surface, and when cool weigh-
ing it, and stamping its value in shillings (reales) upon one
side, and the cross on the other. These coins were called
plata de la cruz—silver of the cross; they are now withdrawn from circulation. In gold there are ounces, half-
ounces, quarters, and eighths, and a new coinage of ten-
dollar pieces called condors and twos. There is also in
copper, the cent and half-cent. Metallic currency has some
disadvantages, for it is heavy, and the silver is incon-
veniently bulky. Large sums are carried in stout linen
bags, and it is common to meet gentlemen in the streets,
with their hands on their way to business, or followed by
peones, carrying the moneybags on their backs.

In Valparaiso there is a banker of immense wealth,
who knows that he is worth $2,000,000, but cannot tell
how much more. He has a small office on one of the principal streets, where I have seen two or three bushels of
ounces on the counter, as he was shoveling them uncounted
into the scales.

XIV

Street Scenes
in Valparaiso

There is a pleasure-garden in the eastern part of the city, much resorted to by all classes—not because the place has many attractions, but because there is no other means of varying the monotony of existence; within this semicircle of hills, where you cannot drive in more than one direction without climbing some acclivity, I always enjoyed my after-dinner rides to the Polanco (as the garden is called), from the novel life I was sure to encounter on the way.

Descending the steep, rocky gorge, by which, from our residence, we reach the streets, we beckon to a passing birlochero, in whose vehicle we seat ourselves with the direction, "Vaya al Polanco," and away we go over the badly paved road at a full gallop. You are jolted against your neighbor, you knock your bonnet against the side, you bound against the top; but you are riding for pleasure, and so grasping a strap, and bracing your feet, you endeavor to enjoy the exercise, consoling yourself with the reflection that it will help you to digest your dinner.

The first person we notice is an old guaso, mounted on a fine horse, with his wife behind him. He wears a bright poncho and straw hat. Her dress is a gay calico, a shawl, and a Panama hat. The horse's bridle is finely plated, with a continuation of the reins fringed at the end—which serves the double purpose of whipping the horse, or lashing any unlucky cur within reach. The bridle bit is powerful enough to break the horse's jaw; and on the saddle are five or six shaggy pillones, or woolen cloths, which almost cover his thighs. The rowels of the guaso's spurs are as large as tea plates; his stirrups are made of a block of carved wood six or eight inches in diameter—forming a complete protection for the feet in passing through rocky gorges and mountain defiles. On one side of the saddle hangs a coiled lasso, made fast to the saddle. The lasso is made of twisted hide about as thick as one's thumb, and some fifty or sixty feet in length, with a slip noose at the end; the mounted guaso is never without it. The skill and precision with which it is thrown is surprising. When the guaso desires to catch an animal while running, he takes the coil of the lasso in his right hand, puts his horse at full speed, and whirling his lasso to give it momentum, hurls its loop around the neck, horns, or leg of the animal, with as much certainty as a skilful ball player sends his ball. The horse is trained, so that the instant the lasso leaves his rider's hand, he stops and braces himself, to bear the strain of the captured animal. The men are bred to this exercise from infancy; and there is not a ragamuffin boy old enough to walk, but is forever practicing his art on poultry, dogs, goats, and sheep, or any small animal that comes in his way. One day, while walking on the Plaza Ancha, we saw one of these little wretches throw his lasso over the head of a passing water carrier, whom he dragged, half choked, from his donkey. The urchin dropped his lasso and ran for life, while the aguador relieved his feelings with all the expletives in the language.

Hurrying onward to the Polanco, we meet and pass other birlochos, gentlemen in gay ponchos, mounted on prancing horses; drunken sailors galloping the street at a breakneck pace, knowing little of horsemanship and caring less; and guasos on mules and donkeys with panniers of fruit and vegetables.

Here is a peon, with a long pole over his shoulder, from which hang bunches of tallow candles (velas de sebo); and there another with a bundle of country brooms, made of broomcorn tied about the end of a rough stick. On our left, we have just passed an hombre, with a number of gay feather dusters made from the plumage of the South American ostrich; just before us is a man carrying two elegant robes of guanaco skins—a soft, fine fur, buff and white, brought from the Straits of Magellan, and used here in winter to rest the feet on; coming toward us is another with a robe of ostrich skins, with gray and white feathers some four inches in length. These are also from the straits, and are used for the same purposes as the guanaco skins.

At the corners, organ-grinders with monkeys, discourse music to the delighted populace—more fortunate than the troubadours of the north, for instead of being continually routed by the police, they are here absolutely paid by the authorities. We pass men seated on the ground, with broad shallow baskets containing cakes and dulces for sale. By and by, as it grows dark, they will light small lanterns, and doze over their wares till bedtime.

Near the garden we cross a bridge that spans a wide deep sewer, now nearly dry, but which, in the rainy season, is a raging torrent. On one side of the *estero* stands a row of mean houses, pulperías, where they sell the liquors of the country; and despachos, where all sorts of meat, vegetables, and fruits may be had. The sidewalks are unpaved, and the doors stand wide open, discovering the filthy earthen floors of the interior, always a little lower than the street—where unwashed, uncombed buyers and sellers are chaffing together, half-naked, squalid children are playing, and fat, greasy women are seated on the ground twangling guitars.

We returned to the city just as a detachment of the police in the Plaza del Orden were being detailed to their different beats for the night. The policemen are divided into two forces, the vigilantes, who preserve order during the day, and the serenos, who watch by night. They are uniformed in coarse blue cloth; a part of each watch is mounted, and are all armed with sabers. The vigilantes go to their beats at daylight, and are authorized to arrest every one violating the peace or public decency, and to keep the streets clean and orderly. One is usually placed at the intersection of every two streets. At twilight the serenos are marched to the relief of the vigilantes. The sereno is never allowed to leave his beat, on any account, until a comrade has responded to his whistle. A house-holder may send him to call a priest or physician, but if either of these reside outside of his district, he must pass the message through his comrades. The sereno examines the street doors of the houses, and if they are not properly secured, he notifies the residents.

After ten o'clock, he cries the hour, describing the weather in a prolonged singsong tone; and the presence of belated persons is announced by whistles, sounding from sereno to sereno, to put all on the alert.

The number and efficiency of the police afford com-parative security; and, on the whole, I think life and property are safer in the midnight streets of Valparaiso than in many cities of the United States. In street en-counters with the disorderly and drunken, the police use their sabers without mercy. In regard to their qualities as censors of cleanliness and decency, they are not so efficient, being ignorant of what cleanliness and decency are, ex-actly.

Dogs are one of the pests of the city. They are of all kinds and colors, from the tiny white Lucia poodle (the pet of the parlor, washed, combed and fleaed every morning), down to the mongrel cur of mangy constitution and un-sightly aspect. They roam about the streets and lie in the doorways; and hundreds that have no masters, live wild on the hills, and gather their food by night from the offal thrown on the beach. One day, to our great horror, a donkey fell dead near our door; but the hungry dogs pounced upon him, and in less than twelve hours no ves-tige of the deceased remained. Of course, the greater part of these dogs belong to the very poor; and every hillside hovel harbors two or three great half-starved brutes, the terror of every passer-by.

XV

Worship and Work

On the 1st of May, the Minister of War died in Valparaiso. From eight o'clock in the morning until sunset, guns were fired every quarter of an hour; and on the day following the minister's death, his remains were taken to the church, where the grand mass was said; the body was then placed in a rich funeral car, drawn by six richly caparisoned black horses, and removed to Santiago, with a numerous escort, as far as the suburbs of Valparaiso, of the military, and the native and foreign officials.

On the 26th of May, the first church building for the Protestant worship in the Republic of Chile, was consecrated at Valparaiso. Catholicism is the established religion of the country, and the law tolerates no other; but there are now so many foreigners resident in Valparaiso that the authorities do not like to interfere in their mode of worship, and are rather disposed to ignore the subject. Our humble edifice was permitted neither bell nor steeple; yet by its architecture it was readily distinguished as a church. Every Sunday, a crowd of the common people gathered around the high board fence that inclosed it, and there was evidently a great deal of curiosity about the forms of heretic devotion. No progress is made in the conversion of the natives to Protestantism; and I do not see how there is to be a change in this respect. If a Bible is presented to a child or adult, the fact is at once made known to the confessor, who of course condemns the book, and bids the penitent beware of the heretic. As in other Catholic countries, the priests here have the strongest hold upon the devout and emotional natures of the women. Many of the educated of the other sex, seeing and feeling the absurdities of the Romish church, are lapsing into infidelity.

In the port at Valparaiso, the Host is now carried to the dying, by a priest with a red umbrella, preceded by three boys with a bell and lighted candle. As the procession passes by, all good Catholics kneel and utter a brief prayer for the departing soul to which the sacred wafer is passing. Formerly, the Host was conveyed with great pomp of military, bells and lights, and was the occasion of constant difficulties between the natives and the heretic foreigners. The authorities finally prohibited these outward demonstrations in the port, but they still continue at the capital and other places. The custom of kneeling as the viático passes, is so sacredly observed, that even the participants in a waltz will pause and bend the knee when the sound of the bell is heard.

Intolerance and superstition, although bad enough in Valparaiso, are unchecked at Santiago. The character of the clergy is low, but they tell their people, "You must live what we preach, not what we practice." They are vowed to celibacy, yet many of them are known to have large families of children; and pretty country cousins are frequent guests at their households. A friend of mine told me that he once attended mass at a town in the interior, where the congregation, impatient at the absence of the priest, sent for his reverence. Their messenger found him at a cockfight, which he refused to leave until the exciting combat was ended. Recently a Chileno died leaving a thousand dollars in the hands of an executor, to be expended in masses for his soul; the native priests would only consent to perform five hundred masses for the money. Accordingly the executor, who had an eye to business, wrote to Spain, and procured a thousand masses for six hundred dollars. The church of Chile then sued him for defrauding it out of its legitimate business.

At the door of every church in Santiago, printed indulgences are for sale on fast days. The usual tenor of the indulgence is, that whoever will observe faithfully certain ceremonies shall have permission to commit minor sins for a specified length of time. The applicant kneels, a lighted candle is placed in his hand, a badge is thrown over his neck, and a priest mutters a prayer. At the close of the ceremony, the applicant rises, pays a dollar, and receives a printed indulgence, with his name written in the blank space, certifying, "In the name of God," that he, ————————, is permitted (for instance) "to eat meat one month during Lent."

Bareheaded friars clothed in coarse woolen gowns, with sandals upon their feet, and carrying a small crucifix, beg from door to door in the cities—presenting the crucifix to be kissed, and expecting a real in return. On the street at the foot of our hill in Valparaiso, is a shop where sacred images are manufactured and sold. The walls are covered with figures of all the saints in the Catholic calendar— varying in size from six inches to six feet. Among the rest was a vivid representation of the Passion of the Saviour— a figure nailed to a cross, with blood starting from the forehead, hands and side.

On the 14th of August, we went by rail a little distance into the country, to dine with a friend who has a contract for building some of the railroad bridges. We found our friend living in a shanty near a gorge in the coast range of mountains, where the grade is very steep, and where five bridges are required within one mile. A large number of peones were at work here, each of whom the contractor paid five reales a day, and furnished with a sufficiency of bread and beans. They had a brush shanty in which to sleep at night; a stone oven to bake their bread, and a large iron kettle to cook their beans. The bread was leavened with yeast; pieces of the dough were weighed, made into loaves, and covered with a dirty poncho, and then placed in the sun to rise. At noon, old nail kegs, filled with cooked beans, were placed on the ground; three or four laborers squatted around each keg, and with a piece of bread in one hand, and in the other a stick flattened at the end, or mussel shell, with which to scoop up the beans, they ate their dinner. When their hunger was satisfied, they threw themselves on the ground, and drew their hats over their eyes for a few moments' siesta. The dress of these peones consisted of a wide pair of cotton drawers, a shirt, and a conical straw hat. The poncho is worn mornings and evenings, and when the weather is cool. At night, it is used for bed covering.

The railroad bridges are very expensive structures. The lumber for their construction is all Norway pine; and the iron girders are brought from England. The piers and abutments are built of very fine granite (resembling the famous Quincy stone), which is found in great abundance near by.

On the "diez y ocho" of this year, I attended grand mass in the church of La Matriz. The building was decorated with flags; and inside, the two rows of pillars were adorned with gay ribbons, and the altar flamed with lighted candles. A soldier stood on guard at each door to prevent the ingress of the lower classes. The church was soon filled with ladies, wearing superb black silks, veils, diamonds, and white gloves, who knelt on mats, spreading their flounced skirts to the utmost extent. We arrived at ten o'clock in the morning; at eleven, the Intendente, with the officers of the army and navy, and the foreign consuls, escorted by military and a band of music, entered the church, and threaded their way through the kneeling groups to the chairs which had been placed for them. The religious ceremonies were similar to those at Santiago, but less imposing. The bishop of Valparaiso officiated. The attendance of military and naval officers at these observances is enforced by the loss of a month's salary for every failure to be present. I was extremely amused by the performances of one of these near me. He was dressed in full uniform and watched the ceremonies very narrowly, lest he should not make his genuflections at the proper time. At his feet was a lady whose skirts covered a vast area, and every time the officer knelt, he planted the end of his sword firmly upon her dress, which she attempted to extricate—so that their time was occupied in the ineffectual struggle. The Danish Consul, whose gorgeous uniform had evidently been made for him when he was a much thinner man, told me that, after kneeling fourteen times, he gave up in despair and exhaustion, and remained quietly seated during the rest of the service.

On the night of the same day, the city was lighted with gas for the first time. At the Plaza Victoria, an inscription was formed of small jets of gas in these words: "Valparaiso, Honor á la ilustre Municipalidad"—Honor to the illustrious Municipality. These the Intendente lighted with his own hand, and then the street jets were lighted.

XVI

Customs and Climate

On the evening of the 28th of September, we experienced the severest shock of earthquake that occurred during our residence in Chile. It came upon us without a premonitory noise or tremor—a tremendous shock that brought us all to our feet in consternation, and rocked the house till every door, window and dish rattled again. With a common impulse we sprang to the door and out upon the hill. Two more shocks followed, each increasing in violence. It was dark, but in the streets below us we could hear the hum of voices, as the people rushed out of their houses, praying to heaven, and calling upon each other; while the dogs added terror to the scene by their doleful howls.

We knew our house to be perfectly safe; an earthquake which could demolish that would destroy the city. Nevertheless, on the slightest tremor of the earth, an irresistible impulse of flight always possessed us.

No buildings were thrown down by this shock, but the walls of many were cracked, and immense damage was done in the fracture of window glass and crockery. The motion of the earthquake seemed to be a perpendicular vibration, like great heavings from beneath; it was felt on the ships in the bay, and produced a heavy swell. During the next twelve days we had nine more, and we seemed in a fair way to be shaken out of our belief that the earth was terra firma. At another time, we had six earthquakes in one week; and in the three years we lived in Chile, we felt fifty-eight shocks. Our nerves became acutely sensitive to the temblor. When all other noises passed unheeded, the faintest roar, or feeblest motion of an earthquake caused us to start and turn pale. Many a time I have been awakened in the night by the trembling of the bedstead— wondered in terror if *that* would amount to any thing, and if the motion did not continue, dropped to sleep again. But if the shock is severe, away you go out of doors, regardless of clothing and propriety, and it is not until the earth is calmed, that you realize your situation. Ridiculous scenes constantly take place; a very severe shock occurred one morning in 1851, just as the American Consul had retired, after his return from a party, to which he had worn his uniform and chapeau. At the first warning he leaped from bed, dashed on his embroidered coat and chapeau, and ran out upon the hill, utterly destitute of pantaloons. Many people will not sleep, nor even sit in a room with closed doors, lest they should be fastened in their frames during an earthquake, and so prevent egress.

The *administrador* of a mine in Copiapó told me that he was once in the depths of the mine, four hundred and fifty yards from the surface, during an earthquake, and that the noise was like that of a thousand gongs, while the motion was scarcely perceptible.

During the three years of our residence in Chile, we had but one thunderstorm, though they are very frequent on the other side of the Andes. Indeed, if one had the arrangement of a climate to suit oneself, one could hardly make one more perfect that that of Chile. In Valparaiso, the mercury ranges from 50° to 80°, and rarely exceeds either extreme. The nights are always cool, and I invariably slept under one heavy blanket, and sometimes two. Thick clothes are always comfortable within doors, and in the shade without.

On account of the coolness of the weather, everybody wears a shawl, and the women have a curious habit of crouching on the floor, with one foot folded under them, in order to keep warm.

From the 1st of April until the 1st of October, "rain may be looked for" in Chile; although the rains frequently do not begin till June, and cease in August. After that, as certainly as the day dawns, the sun shines.

The people here are divided into two classes: the gentry, and the peones or peasants. Of the former class, the men are rather below the medium size. They invariably have black hair and eyes—with a sallow complexion which is sometimes very dark. Many of them are well educated in the Chileno schools and colleges, and a few have traveled in Europe or the United States; but they are indolent and effeminate, never doing today what can be done tomorrow—fond of gaming and dress—inveterate smokers, and loose in their notions of morality.

The beauty of the women has been greatly overrated. When they wore the graceful black veil, which harmonized so well with their jet-black hair and eyes, they had attractions which they do not possess now, when dressed in colors. As they approach middle life, they incline to flesh. They are indolent and slovenly. The Chileno lady rises late; she dresses hastily, throwing a charitable shawl about her to hide manifold sins of omission. Her little feet are carelessly thrust into slippers, her hair is plaited in two braids that fall down her back. Her ablutions are merely a form of politeness to the washbowl. In this dishabille she dawdles about, amusing herself with some fancy work, until ennui drives her to seek refuge in shopping or paying visits. Then she makes her appearance in all the splendor of silks and diamonds, never wearing muslin or calico, and preferring a tattered silk for morning dress, to the most exquisite cotton fabric.

Servants are abundant, and if one does not please, a better may be had; so that the ladies here are relieved entirely of one of the most harassing responsibilities of northern housekeepers. A young girl never leaves the house of her parents unless accompanied by some member of the family or a female servant. If she pays a visit, the duenna waits for her at the front door, or gossips with the other servants. Interviews between young ladies and gentlemen never take place except in the presence of others. Of course, marriages of convenience are frequent. There are also many instances of matrimony within the forbidden degrees of consanguinity—even to the union of uncles with nieces, and stepfathers with stepdaughters. The honeymoon is passed in strict seclusion; after that, the husband and wife usually occupy separate apartments.

Children at birth are almost invariably given in charge to a wet nurse, whose child in turn is nursed by a poorer woman. This nurse of the nurse's child, in nine cases out of ten, has never been married.

Some of the social customs of the Chilenos are peculiar. Hospitality to evening visitors is expressed in tea and cakes—the hostess always pouring out the beverage, and a servant passing it to the guests. Yerba mate, the leaves of a shrub imported from Paraguay, is the beverage of the common people, and is also much used by the better classes; though the Chinese plant takes its place in the parlor. The yerba mate has the taste of tea, with a faint savor of tobacco, and is a slightly exhilarating drink. It is always prepared with sugar in the dish, from which it is drunk, or sucked, boiling hot, through a tube. The poor use little gourds with a bamboo tube called a bombilla, while the rich indulge in elegant chased silver or china cups, with a bombilla of silver.

Evening parties (tertulias) are much in fashion, the refreshments being usually cakes, ices and tea.

Thirty years ago, the Chilenos welcomed all foreigners with overflowing hospitality, and with a primitive warmth and simplicity that was delightful. Such welcome is now seldom shown, except in remote places in the country, where the mate cup with its bombilla is still passed from your neighbor's lips, no matter how old or ugly, to your own; and where your hostess will pause in front of you, with her dish of dulces in one hand and spoon in the other, while she envelopes a peach in its syrup to gently thrust it into your expectant mouth, and so pass on around the circle. Now, letters of introduction, although not absolutely necessary, still facilitate your entrance into society. A gentleman leaves his card for you, and at your first visit will "celebrate greatly acquaintance with you," and assures you "that the house and all it contains are wholly at your service"—high-sounding but meaningless phrases, though it is true that you have the entreé of his house, where his wife will receive you cordially. The saloon is always lighted at evening, where you can drop in without knocking, at nine or ten, to take tea, and remain until midnight, or perhaps later; music, conversation, and tea are the amusements. The gentleman of the house is not often present, spending his evenings with other companions, and perhaps in not so innocent a manner. Sunday is the day for complimentary visiting, calls being made at two or three in the afternoon, and also at twilight. Ladies are rarely attended home from evening visits by any one but a servant, custom not permitting beaux to accompany them, unless affianced, and then with the servant also. Acquaintances always address each other by the given name, with the prefix of Don, Doña, or Señorita, an affectionate custom much less ceremonious than our own.

The tender love between mother and daughter, as it exists with us, is unknown. The child being at birth intrusted to a wet nurse, goes later to school, where she sees her mother but seldom; she is constantly under the care of servants, and there can be but little confidence between them, which the confessional probably lessens. If she wishes sympathy or advice she goes to a companion, looking upon her mother, who should be her best friend, as her natural enemy. Never mingling with boys at school, and when grown, never enjoying freely the society of the other sex, she is ignorant of her own powers of pleasing or conversation. In nine cases out of ten, married without consulting her wishes, she is an indifferent wife of an unfaithful husband. In religion she is willing to be guided solely by her confessor, without consulting her own judgment. The intellect of the females I think superior to that of the male sex, but in Chile there is little to excite their ambition. There are no lectures, no literary societies, but few cultivated minds to come in contact with. There is no opportunity of traveling in their own country, except up and down the coast to a few miserable ports, and back and forth from Valparaiso to Santiago. Both sexes confess to apathy. "Personal labor is considered degrading. Want of occupation encouraged by the climate soon confirms a habit of indolence, where there is no mental energy to shake it off, and in a brief while the youth, who might have become a man of ability and enterprise, falls irreclaimably into idleness and listlessness." Thus life is one monotonous round—to the female, of going to mass in the morning, attending to a few domestic duties during the day, and the opera or a tertulia in the evening. The male sex omit the mass, look a little after their business affairs if they have any, go to the opera or tertulia, or the gaming table for the night.

Ladies never attend funerals. Within ten days after the obsequies, it is customary to pay visits of condolence. The mourners for many days sit in one corner of a darkened parlor, and the first arrivals seat themselves next the afflicted, expressing sympathy for the living, or regret for the dead; then make their bows and retire, as the succeeding arrivals move up.

Gambling is a national vice; but the miners carry it on more extensively than any other class. One instance came under my own observation where the proprietor of a mine, on a steamer coming down from Copiapó, lost ninety thousand dollars in a single night. At many of the houses in Santiago the gaming table is regularly set out, and forms one of the features at their entertainments. The poorest peones and raggedest urchins can be seen at any time in the lanes and alleys, betting *medios* and *centavos* with as much eagerness as the miner does his ounces. There are laws against gaming, but they are not enforced, and even the Church keeps silent, as many of her dignitaries are experienced *monte* players.

Although all titles are abolished, many of the old families would be proud to retain them, and still keep up the retinue and state of nobility. The Countess de Toro, whom I saw at Santiago, pays the government a yearly sum for the privilege of being called countess—an empty gratification for which she can well afford to pay, for her wealth is almost fabulous. At a ball given during the festivities of the "diez y ocho," besides being richly dressed, she wore diamonds estimated to be worth forty thousand dollars. She sports a Parisian coach-and-four, with four outriders and a postillion. Her house is a large, two-story brick mansion, painted a brilliant red, with white doors and window casings. Her husband *ordered* in his will that the color should remain unchanged, and the slightest deviation would forfeit the property.

In the country, on the large estates, many of the hacendados live in almost regal style, keeping large retinues of servants and troops of horses with which to serve and amuse the guests, with whom they are always happy to have their houses filled.

We profess to be a cultivated people and stiffen our necks with Yankee independence, but in some things we might learn courtesty from the Chilenos. They never enter or leave a public vehicle without a bow to its occupants, and we never make one unless to an acquaintance. At the table d'hote at the hotel in Santiago, no lady or gentleman ever sat down, or rose from table without a graceful inclination of the head to all who were present. So in shopping, they bow to the merchant or his clerks on entering and leaving the store. These simple acts of politeness always impressed me pleasantly, and as so much better than our own don't-care-for-any-body sort of way. In the street, however, the Chilenos might learn from us. If a group of gentlemen are conversing on the narrow sidewalk, and a lady approaches, they often will not notice her, or will perhaps step back, leaving her the curbstone. Sometimes she is obliged to step into the gutter to pass around them.

No place except the church is sacred from the fumes of the cigar. Gentlemen, whether riding or walking, with or without ladies, are always smoking. The priest in the Pantheon takes a whiff between prayers; and even the firemen while running with their engines, must pause to light the cigarrito, let the urgency be ever so great. The señoritas have the name of being addicted to this habit, and I was told that formerly the greatest compliment a lady could pay a gentleman was to light the cigarrito and pass it to him from her own lips; but I never saw any thing of this.

This is life in Chile. To vegetate in a soft climate, free from excitement, except an occasional revolution, or earthquake; to attend strictly all the fiestas of holy church, and ensure salvation, as the priests say; to walk in the evening in the alamedas or public gardens (termed in their grandiloquent style, jardines de las delicias—gardens of delight), and to enjoy the moonlight, as advertised in the daily paper, Esta noche tendrán oportunidad las hermosas señoritas de pasearse en el Eden, y oir encantado la música bajo la luna de enero. (This evening our fair ladies will have the opportunity of promenading in the enchanted Eden, and listening to music beneath the light of the January moon.)

As to the second and poorer class of the Chilenos, the peones are hideously ugly—with thick heads of hair hanging straight from the crown, high cheekbones, wide mouths, and copper-colored complexions. Small hands and feet are property in the beautiful, common to all Chilenos. Some of the women of the peones are quite pretty, but there is a great want of chastity among them. Unions without marriage are frequent, and are excused on the ground that the blessing of the church is too great an expense to be incurred. Born as inferiors and dependents, the highest ambition of the peones is to serve masters or mistresses of wealth and consequence, addressing them as Patrón, and Patrona. Their necessities are few, and may be summed up in a mud, or adobe hut, a hide in one corner upon which to sleep, an iron pot and mate cup, bread and beans for substantial food, with garlic, or onions and fruits for relishes. In the cool rains of winter they shiver uncomplainingly, and when the sun shines, crouch into every sheltered nook and corner to enjoy its grateful warmth. Like all ignorant people they are superstitious, believing in charms and amulets as powerful to drive away diseases; and it is common to see them with little round plasters upon their temples as antidotes for headache. On Sundays they visit the barber, who is one of their own class, and whose shop is the shady side of a bit of cloth stretched upon poles; and there perform their toilet for the week to come. The wages of a year's labor is often spent upon a poncho to wear at the "diez y ocho." Mechanics and shopkeepers are a degree removed from these, but there is a want of cleanliness in all; and a passion for display and finery that, to gratify in public, they will suffer any deprivation at home.

The 1st of November is All-Saints Day, when in Catholic countries, surviving friends decorate the graves of the dead, and procure prayers to be said for the souls of the departed. The road leading to the Pantheon at Valparaiso, on this day was thronged with people in deep black, on their way to the performance of these rites. The cemetery had been put in order for the occasion—the pits had been filled up, and the pieces of coffins and bones had been cleared away. We passed through aisles of beggars on the hillside to the gates of the Pantheon, where vendors of fruits, cakes, ices, and milk punch, hoarsely offered their wares to purchase, while the vigilantes, running about to preserve order, contributed to a scene of confusion more appropriate to the entrance of a fair ground than the solemn abode of the dead. At the portal of the Pantheon is a hall opening upon a corridor, near which the chapel was filled with kneeling devotees. The interior was draped with black, and lamps were burning before the altar. In front of the chapel was a table on which stood a figure of the Saviour, with an old, brown skull, surrounded with wax tapers at its feet.

The monuments and tombstones were all covered with fresh flowers, in wreaths, festoons, and vases, while blossoms were lavishly scattered upon the graves. Many tombs were adorned with beautiful garlands of immortelles. Groups of people chatting gaily were seated upon the stones, while at various points throughout the grounds, priests of different orders were repeating prayers for the dead. Passing down the broad walk, on my left was a reverend man in long robes of black broadcloth, who would pray for any desired soul, at one *real* a prayer; while on the left was a portly-looking person in a flowing gown of white merino, whose supplications came one *real* higher. Beyond these were two priests in gray cloth, who looked rather seedy. Their demand was one penny, and to these the very poor came, untying the coin from the corner of a handkerchief, while one of the priests muttered the prayer for which it was to pay. Meanwhile a person in secular costume, followed by a score of women, went from cross to cross at the graves of the poor, petitioning the Virgin in their behalf.

XVII

CONCEPCIÓN

Our last summer in Chile was the warmest we experienced in that climate—the thermometer in the shade rising several times as high as 78°.

We had made up our minds to quit Valparaiso during the month of February, with the intention of returning home by way of Cape Horn, instead of crossing the Isthmus again—for two reasons: the one was that the Isthmus route was very expensive, and the other that a detention of two weeks, either at Panama or Aspinwall, was unavoidable, and afforded opportunities for taking the Panama fever altogether too flattering.

A line of ships, between Boston and Valparaiso, made regular trips, and we determined to take passage in one of these. Our ship was to return to the United States with a cargo of wool and copper ores, going to Coquimbo for the latter, and thence down the coast, below Valparaiso, to the ports of Tomé, and Talcahuano, in the Bay of Concepción, for the wool—not touching at our port on her downward passage. So we took the propeller "Valdivia," and joined her at Talcahuano.

We left Valparaiso with many regrets, for our residence in its soft climate, and amid its novel scenes had been most agreeable, and we were parting moreover from many kind friends. On the 10th of February, at noon, we rounded the lighthouse point, and shut the familiar bay and city from our view. The second night, at eight o'clock, we reached Tomé, lying at anchor all night, and early in the morning crossing six miles to Talcahuano. The Bay of Concepción, is six miles long and four miles wide, with Tomé, Liriguen, and Penco on the east, and Talcahuano on the west. At the entrance lies the island of Quiriguina, nearly three miles in length, and one in width. Talcahuano was entirely destroyed by an earthquake and the sea, on the 20th of February in 1835. The sea receded and then advanced in three successive waves—unbroken walls of water, thirty feet in height—dragging ships from their anchors, and dashing one more than two hundred yards inland—sweeping houses from their foundations, and in the subsidence, bearing away the ruins, and leaving the site of the town desolate. At the first alarm, the inhabitants fled to the hills behind the town, and there, with the earth quaking so violently beneath them that it was impossible to stand, they beheld the advance of the devouring sea, and the utter destruction of their property. Talcahuano now contains about four thousand inhabitants, and like other South American towns, is mostly built of adobes, though there are some framed and brick houses in the place. It has narrow streets, and one plaza, where you wander about in the dust, amid peones, donkeys, dogs, and fleas, and behold women sitting in their doorways, strumming guitars.

It is a great resort for whale ships in the summer season, and of course the streets abound in drunken sailors whom you always see in a disturbance of some kind.

One day while there, the sound of music attracted me to my door, when I witnessed a most singular pageant. A peon was carrying on his extended hands a board about five feet long, upon which lay the body of an infant, dressed in pink. The eyes stood wide open, and the cheeks were painted to simulate the flush of health. The man was followed first by two women, then by two men—one playing a fiddle and the other a guitar—while a halfscore of both sexes, brought up the rear, gaily laughing and chatting together. They were going to bury the angelita, over whom they had danced and frolicked for three days— perhaps *lending* it, in the mean time, once or twice to some family that were not so fortunate as to have a corpse of their own; and so furnishing an excuse for orgies quite as wild and ridiculous as those of an Irish wake. This custom is generally observed among the more degraded classes, who often keep a corpse for festive purposes until it becomes offensive to all who approach the house.

Here, as at Valparaiso, ships are unladen and laden by means of launches. The boatmen are a class who follow this business and no other. The launch is rowed near the beach, and then pushed on it, stern foremost, as far as the depth of the water will permit; the men, naked save for a shirt and a piece of cloth about the loins, wade through the surf carrying articles to shore, no matter what their size or weight. I have seen twelve of these men bring to shore in this way a large carriage boxed up. Their muscular frames become wonderfully developed, and it is astonishing with what rapidity they perform their work.

Concepción, formerly called Penco, was situated on the eastern side of the bay, but its repeated destruction by earthquakes, the sea, and the Araucanian Indians, drove the inhabitants nine miles inland, where they located the present city, upon the northern bank of the river Bío-Bío, a large navigable stream.

Old Penco, as it is now called, possesses peculiar interest from its historical associations, for it was here that the cross was first raised in southern Chile, by General Valdivia, in 1550. All that is now to be seen of its former greatness are the remains of an old fort, or water battery, with walls of great extent and six feet in thickness. On the façade is cut in stone the Spanish coat of arms, covering a space of eight feet square, with the date, "Año 1687."

The road from Talcahuano to Concepción traverses a sandy plain, dotted here and there with shrubs and dwarf trees. As we approached, at first we saw what seemed a few scattering huts, at the base of a range of sand hills, and not far off, the river Bío-Bío; and were surprised soon afterwards to find ourselves in the midst of a city of some twelve thousand inhabitants. The streets are of moderate width, and the buildings are of course like those of all other Chileno towns. It was noon when we entered the city, and in passing through a long street to our hotel, we saw only three animated objects—two men and a donkey.

It was the hour of the siesta, the whole city was asleep, and in broad day, amid so many thousands of people, there was utter silence.

The great earthquake of 1835 destroyed Concepción. A lady, who resided there at the time, told me that but one house was left standing, and that she lived for some time afterwards in a tent. The stone Cathedral of the city has never been rebuilt; its foundation walls on one side, and the archway of the door alone remain.

I may describe the Hotel del Sur, for it was like all other houses of the kind in Chile. There was a passage in the center, through which the donkeys with wood and water were driven to the kitchen. The only room to sit in was the dining room, floored with brick, and with a bar of liquors in one corner. The bedrooms opened on the patio. The kitchen, about twelve feet square, had a brick range on one side, and a table opposite—the floor of earth, plastered over with all the grease and victuals that had been dropped upon it during the preparation of innumerable dinners.

The province of Concepción is of untold fertility; it produces enormous quantities of wheat of the finest quality, and barley, beans, and vegetables of every description, as well as fruits and wine, and cattle and sheep. A wine called musto, which they make here in large quantities, is like Burgundy in flavor. From the forests of apple trees that grow without culture, the national drink chicha is made, and a pine tree on the slopes of the Andes yields the piñon, a nut similar to the chestnut when boiled, and prized as a delicacy by the ladies of Santiago, while to the Araucanians, it is bread.

Gold, copper, and coal abound, and only enterprise and mining intelligence are needed to develop vast mineral resources.

As soon as the rains have sufficiently softened the ground, it is prepared for wheat by the rude plough of the natives, a knee-shaped piece of wood, of which the larger end serves as the share, and the smaller as the handle. It has a second straight beam near the joint for the tongue, and the end of the share is shod with iron. It does not make a furrow more than six inches in depth. The oxen are attached by means of a long straight yoke lashed to their horns. Ploughs have been brought from the United States and England, but the laborers will only use them while under the eye of the proprietor, and are averse to innovations and improvements. The grain is sown broadcast, and covered by dragging brush over it; and the sickle is used for reaping.

While in Concepción I had an opportunity of witnessing the labors of the wheat threshing, which is an annual event of great importance. As the wheat is cut, it is placed in a pile on an elevated site, until it rises to the height of a considerable hill. The pile I saw was as large as six of our common hayricks, and was inclosed by a high fence of poles and bushes, adjoining a field in which were some forty mares, only used in this country for the purpose of increasing the stock. A portion of the grain was thrown from the pile upon the ground; the mares, with a half-dozen guasos to drive them, were turned in, and at a signal from the mayordomo, stationed on the summit of the pile—away they went at full speed, incited by the whips of their drivers, and the yells of a crowd of men and boys outside. After a certain number of rounds, "Vuelta!" roared the mayordomo, when the mares turned in their tracks and ran in an opposite direction—half obscured in straw and clouds of dust. Now and then one lost her footing and fell, of course bringing all behind her to a full stop, but doing no injury to herself in the mass of straw. When exhausted, the mares are turned into the corral to rest, while the grain was scraped up near the fence, and a new supply of unthreshed ears scattered over the ground. After the grain is threshed, it is winnowed by being tossed into the air, with shovels, when the wind blows away the chaff. On some haciendas, where the crop of wheat is large, one or two hundred mares are employed in the threshing, a sufficient number being hired from neighboring estates, when there are not enough on the proprietor's farm. A daily feast for the laborers in provided by the patrón as long as the trilla lasts. It is difficult to arrive accurately at the amount of wheat raised in Concepción, but the average value of the crop is something near $12,000,000.

The bean crop, of which there are some sixteen varieties, is of more importance to the laboring classes than any other—that vegetable constituting their chief article of diet. Indian corn does not thrive well, and beans supply to a great extent the place of bread.

XVIII

THE ARAUCANIANS

The southern part of Chile is classic ground. There, inhabiting a delightful territory, situated between the rivers Bío-Bío and Valdivia, and between the Andes and the sea, extending from 30° 44′ to 34° 50′, south latitude, is a nation of Indians, named by the Spaniards, Araucanos, who have maintained their independence for more than three centuries. So strenuous and successful has been their resistance, that their country was early called, by their invaders, the "Invincible State," and a Spanish poet has magnanimously celebrated in epic poetry the exploits of a people, who, to preserve their independence, have caused such torrents of Spanish blood to flow.

The Spaniards, under their great general, Pedro de Valdivia, having conquered the northern provinces, and founded the cities of Santiago and Concepción, in 1550, crossed the Bío-Bío to give the Araucanians battle. After a hard contest, in which Valdivia said "he was never in such imminent hazard of his life," the Indians, losing their chief, retreated, and left the Spaniards too much exhausted to pursue them.

For the next few years, owing to the timidity of the Indian commander, Valdivia, sometimes defeated and at others victorious, advanced into their territory and founded seven cities, which prospered for a time. The Araucanos finally deposing their old chief, elected Caupolicán, who renewed the war, and prosecuted it with vigor, besieging cities and destroying fortifications, until the inhabitants, driven from one place to another, at last narrowly escaped in a vessel from Valdivia.

Deeds of heroism done in this war are recorded worthy of more civilized nations. The Araucanos, in their deadly hatred of the Spaniards and their determination to keep their country free from the yoke of the foreigners, who, under the plea of spreading their religion, committed every cruelty and oppression that human nature could invent, continued hostilities with a perseverance and resoluteness of purpose which nothing could turn aside.

"In a battle between Caupolicán and Valdivia, when victory seemed in favor of the Spaniards, a young Indian named Lautaro, but sixteen years of age, whom Valdivia had taken in one of his incursions, baptized and made his page, quitted the victorious party, reproached his countrymen with cowardice, and grasping a lance, turned against his late master, crying out, 'Follow me, my countrymen; victory courts us with open arms.'

"The Araucanians, ashamed at being surpassed by a boy, turned with such fury upon their enemies as to put them to rout and destroy them, so that of the whole army but two escaped."

Valdivia was taken prisoner and killed in 1553, and as years passed on, was succeeded by other generals, and Caupolicán had many successors.

Caupolicán was the most distinguished of all the Araucanian chiefs. He was defeated in battle, and for a long time his retreat was unknown, but finally one of the natives being severely tortured, revealed his hiding place, when he was captured, after a terrific struggle, with ten of his followers, who would not abandon him. His wife, who exhorted him to die rather than surrender, on seeing him taken, threw her infant son at his feet, saying, "She would retain nothing that belonged to a coward."

In 1590, the Indian chief Guepotán, who had for a long time defended a pass in the Andes, desiring to have his wife with him, descended into the plains in search of her, but was surprised by a party of Spaniards and killed.

His wife, Janequeo, burning with a desire to revenge her husband's death, placed herself, with her brother, at the head of a company of neighboring Indians, and made inroads into the Spanish settlements, killing all who fell into her hands.

She sustained successfully many contests with an experienced Spanish general, and at the commencement of the rainy season retired to the mountains, fortifying herself in a place surrounded by precipices; from whence she daily harassed a neighboring city in such a manner that no one dared to leave it. She was finally driven from her stronghold by artillery, and saved herself by flight.

For ninety years the Indians, armed only with spears, lances, bows and arrows, waged war with their invaders, who were supplied with firearms, and constantly recruited from Peru.

Finally the Spanish government, seeing it had made but little progress in conquering this fierce and warlike people, made a treaty of peace with them, which continued until 1655, when war again broke out, continuing with violence for ten years.

After an interval of peace, in 1723, the Araucanians determined to expel the Spaniards from the whole of Chile, but this war only amounted to a few skirmishes, when peace was established.

The Araucanians are of medium height, muscular, and well formed, with a reddish-brown complexion; their faces are oval, with small expressive eyes, rather flat noses, and white, even teeth; the hair, coarse and black, is worn long by both sexes, and wound in tresses around the head. They have many virtuous qualities as well as savage vices, and a haughty contempt for all other nations. The dress of the men consists of shirt, pantaloons, and poncho, of coarse woollen cloth. The women wear a tunic, and ornaments of gold; silver and beads are much prized among them.

Polygamy exists, and plurality of wives are employed in manufacturing cloth and ponchos—the latter often of delicate fineness, embroidered with figures of flowers and animals, and worth a hundred and fifty dollars.

The art of weaving was understood by them before the arrival of the Europeans in the country, and they had the same style of plough now used by the Chilenos.

The interior of their territory is almost unknown, as they are so suspicious of the white race, that only peddlers, bringing toys and finery, are permitted to pass to the plains. From them we learn that the country is well watered by large rivers, has fine forests of timber in the interior, and is rich in mines of gold, silver, salt, and coal; that they have immense herds of cattle and horses to barter for trinkets—orchards of apples and pears, adjoined by fields of wheat, barley, beans, and cabbage; and that their houses are built of mud or reeds, and situated near streams of water.

The cities founded by Valdivia (of which Imperial was the finest), with the exception of the one bearing his name, have been for more than two centuries an undistinguishable mass of ruins. Valdivia, built upon a river of the same name, eight miles from the sea, is now a German colony under the auspices of the Chilean government, and although the colonists are provided with arms for defense, the Indians occasionally rush in and lay the whole city under contribution. It is said that they can bring ten thousand warriors into the field, and being most expert riders, they generally fight on horseback. Catholic missionaries are scattered among the savages along the coast, but they make but little progress.

Mention the Araucanians to a Chileno at this day and he will turn pale; and I was informed that the government gave them a large subsidy to keep the peace.

A niece of a well-known family in Valparaiso, some years since, started down the coast for Valdivia in an old, crazy vessel, much against the wishes of her friends. The vessel was wrecked—she fell into the hands of the Indians, and is the wife now of one of their chiefs. One thousand gold ounces has been offered by the Chile government as her ransom, but they refused to give her up at any price.

President Montt, the present Executive, was making a tour in the south of Chile, and sent word for one of their caciques to come and see him. "Tell Montt," he replied, "if he wants to see me, to come where I am,"—showing that the proud spirit of the great Caupolicán is not yet extinct in that people.

XIX

Homeward Bound

Our voyage to Boston was not marked by any other than the usual events of voyages by the Cape Horn route. We set sail from the Bay of Talcahuano, on the 23d of February. On the 3d of March, a strong gale commenced blowing, with occasional squalls of snow, and during a storm of two days, we learned how angry a Pacific ocean may become. By the 7th, we were seventy-seven miles south of Cape Horn, and after a calm of six hours, our ship headed homeward with a fair strong wind, making for several days two hundred and twenty-five miles every twenty-four hours. The weather was cold and disagreeable; and to this I had the added horrors of seasickness.

We saw the albatross, and the Cape pigeon, and as we entered warmer latitudes, flying fish began to make their appearance; and stormy petrels flashed eagerly around the ship, and fed on the bits of pork thrown to them.

On Sunday morning, while we were at breakfast, the man at the wheel gave an alarm of sharks, and we hurried to the deck. In the water about the stern, some thirty of these hideous monsters were playing. They were from three to seven feet in length, with smooth backs of dark green color, and white bellies. A shark hook was quickly baited with a pound or two of pork, and thrown over, when one of the largest sharks seized it. He was dragged on board by the sailors, and was duly tormented by his implacable enemies.

As we approached the equator, the fine winds which had wafted us so far, died away, and in one week we only made one hundred and seventeen miles. The indolent, careless life of the calm was pleasant enough. We brought our books and work to the deck, and, under an awning which had been put up to screen us from the sun, watched the sailors painting and repairing the rigging. The demon of seasickness was laid for the time. Sky above and sea below were deliciously blue; the slow sun rose and sank; the moon nightly poured her light upon the smooth and silent ocean, while the sailors sang their songs, and talked of every land. We ate and slept; we lived in our little lazy city of wooden walls, and knew nothing of the toil and turmoil of the great worlds to the east and west.

One night, when we were within three miles of the equator, I was awakened by the sound of the ship rushing through the water. A fair wind was blowing, and we were once more in flight for home.

Every night we examined the chart to see how rapidly the distance between us and home decreased, and grew more impatient as we drew nearer to our native land. In the gulf stream we had one rough day, but after that, our progress was rapid and almost direct.

Ho, for land! When seventy-six days out, the Captain announced that, on the morrow at two, we should see Cape Cod. That day the sun rose brightly; the wind blew fresh and free, and our ship carried every stitch of canvas her masts would bear.

As the hour of two approached, all eyes were turned in eager expectation. "Land ho! Land ho!" shouts the lookout from aloft. "Land ho!" echoes the Captain, and all who can, mount the rigging.

It is not long before my unpractised eyes distinguish the sandy hills of Cape Cod, and my heart leaps with a joyful rapture to behold my native land once more.

At eight o'clock we enter Boston Harbor, and in fifteen minutes, a pilot takes us up the channel.